MUTUAL REMINDING

﹆

GOOD MANNERS

THE WRITINGS OF IMĀM AL-ḤADDĀD

TWO TREATISES

MUTUAL REMINDING

❧

GOOD MANNERS

IMĀM ʿABDALLĀH IBN ʿALAWĪ AL-ḤADDĀD

Translated by
MOSTAFA AL-BADAWI

THE STARLATCH PRESS

©2002 by Mostafa al-Badawi. All rights reserved. No part of this book may be reproduced, stored, or transmitted in any form or by any means, electronic or otherwise, including photocopying, recording, Internet, or any storage and retrieval system without prior written permission from the Starlatch Press.™

Printed in the United States of America.

11 10 09 08 07 06 05 04 03 02   10 9 8 7 6 5 4 3 2 1

ISBN: 1-929694-17-2 (Sewn Softcover)

Starlatch Press
phone: (708) 599-0909
fax: (708) 570-0758
www.starlatch.com
info@starlatch.com

This book is printed on premium acid-free paper that meets the minimum requirements set for alkaline papers by the American National Standard for Information Sciences—Permanence of paper for printed Library Materials, ANSI Z 39.48-1984.

TRANSLITERATION KEY

ء	ʾ (1)	ر	r (6)	ف	f
ا	ā, a	ز	z	ق	q (13)
ب	b	س	s	ك	k
ت	t	ش	sh	ل	l
ث	th (2)	ص	ṣ (7)	م	m
ج	j	ض	ḍ (8)	ن	n
ح	ḥ (3)	ط	ṭ (9)	ه	h (14)
خ	kh (4)	ظ	ẓ (10)	و	ū, u, w
د	d	ع	ʿ (11)	ي	ī, i, y
ذ	dh (5)	غ	gh (12)		

ﷺ—Mentioned after the Prophet Muḥammad's ﷺ name and translated as "may Allah bless him and grant him peace."

عليه السلام—Mentioned after the names of the prophets and translated as "peace be upon him."

---

1. A distinctive glottal stop made at the bottom of the throat. It is also used to indicate the running of two words into one, e.g. *bismi'Llāh*.
2. Should be pronounced like the *th* in think.
3. A hard *h* sound made at the Adam's apple in the middle of the throat.
4. Pronounced like the *ch* in Scottish loch.
5. Should be pronounced like the *th* in this.
6. A slightly trilled *r* made behind the front teeth which is trilled not more than twice.
7. An emphatic *s* pronounced behind the upper front teeth.
8. An emphatic *d*-like sound made by pressing the entire tongue against the upper palate.
9. An emphatic *t* sound produced behind the front teeth.
10. An emphatic *th* sound, like the *th* in this, made behind the front teeth.
11. A distinctive Semitic sound made in the middle throat and sounding to a Western ear more like a vowel than a consonant.
12. A guttural sound made at the top of the throat resembling the untrilled German and French *r*.
13. A hard *k* sound produced at the back of the palate.
14. This sound is like the English *h* but has more body. It is made at the very bottom of the throat and pronounced at the beginning, middle, and ends of words.

CONTENTS

TRANSLATOR'S INTRODUCTION — IX

MUTUAL REMINDING

	PROLOGUE	3
1	The Meaning of Taqwā	6
2	The Recompense of Works	7
3	God's Satisfaction and His Wrath	9
4	The Reward of the Pious	10
5	The Abasement of the Corrupt	12
6	Delight in Obedience	14
7	The Four Obstacles to Obedience	15
8	Ignorance	16
9	Weakness of Faith	17
10	Long Hopes	18
11	Illicit and Suspect Food	20
12	Sincerity	21
13	Ostentation	21
14	Conceit	22
15	Love of this World	23
	CONCLUSION	23
	AFTERWORD	36
	NOTES	41

GOOD MANNERS

	PROLOGUE	47
1	The Beginning of the Path: a Powerful Urge of Divine Origin Which Should be Strengthened, Protected, and Responded To	49
2	Repentance: Its Conditions, and Protecting Oneself from Sins	50
3	Guarding the Heart Against Insinuations, Ailments, and Ill-Thinking	51
4	Guarding the Senses Against Transgressions and Against being Deceived by This World	54

5	Remaining in a State of Purity and Preferring Hunger to Satiety	55
6	Directing One's Whole Attention to God and Devoting Oneself to His Worship	56
7	Excellence in the Performance of Ritual Prayers, Presence with God is the Essence of All Acts of Worship	57
8	Caution Against Neglecting the Friday Prayer and Other Congregational Prayers, Exhortation to Perform the Regular Supererogatory Prayers	58
9	Exhortation to Persevere in Remembrance and Reflection	59
10	How to Rebuke the Soul from being Lazy in Obedience and Inclined Towards Disobedience	61
11	The States of the Soul and Patience	61
12	Heeding the Example of the People of Fortitude—Provision is Apportioned	62
13	Moving Toward God being Compatible with Earning, Divesting Oneself of the Means of Livelihood is Not Required	64
14	Being Patient when Harmed by Others and being Wary of Tempted by Them	65
15	Getting Rid of the Need to Obtain Other People's Approval	66
16	Rebuking the Seekers of Unveilings and Supernatural Events	66
17	The Seeking of Provision and Striving for It	67
18	Keeping the Company of the Best of People, the Good Manners of the Disciple with His Shaykh, and the Attributes of the Perfect Shaykh	68
	CONCLUSION	71
	NOTES	75
	TRANSLATOR'S APPENDIX ONE	77
	TRANSLATOR'S APPENDIX TWO	79

TRANSLATOR'S INTRODUCTION

In the name of God, the All-Merciful, the Compassionate

The Prophet ﷺ said, "He who believes in God and the Last Day, let him speak words of goodness or else remain silent." In another tradition, we learn what is meant here by "words of goodness." He said, "The speech of the Son of Adam will be counted against him, not for him, except for enjoining good, forbidding evil, and remembering God." When a Muslim meets another, this should be the matter of their discourse. Obviously, they must exchange greetings of peace, inquire about each other's health, family, and other affairs; for this keeps the bonds of brotherly affection alive. But having done so, they should turn to reminding each other of that which brings the fragrance of faith in their lives and renders, by God's will, their life-to-come successful.

As for the learnéd men and women of the Muslim nation, they are the ones primarily intended by God's command: *And remind, for reminding profits the believers* (QURAN, 51:55). Who is better qualified than these learnéd and godly people to obey this order and strive to carry it out with substance, wisdom, and befitting ways?

Imām ʿAbdallāh al-Ḥaddād was such a learnéd man. His was a

life infused with the love of and unrivaled capacity to remind Muslims of God, His Messenger, and the Last Day. His very presence was a constant reminder to those around him, as well as to those who only heard or read about his counsel of how a Muslim should behave toward his Lord and his brother Muslim.

The first of the two concise books contained in this volume is known as *The Treatise of Mutual Reminding among Loving Brothers, People of Goodness and Religion*. It was the Imām's first work, dictated in 1069 AH when he was twenty-five years of age. In it he examines mutual reminding and the exchange of good counsel, and he identifies its chief elements as *taqwā* (an active consciousness and fear of God)[1] and detachment from worldly things. He defines *taqwā* according to the criteria of Imām al-Ghazālī and delineates both its active aspect of doing good and its passive aspect of avoiding evil. He then discusses the four things that impair it (ignorance, weakness of faith, long hopes, and illicit and dubious sustenance). He goes on next to discuss two of the major obstacles on the path of obedience, namely, conceit and ostentation, both of which seriously assail one's sincerity. Finally, he speaks of how the love of this world severs one from God, quoting numerous Quranic verses, Prophetic traditions, and sayings of the virtuous predecessors among the early and venerable Muslim generations.

Taqwā and detachment from the world naturally lead to seeking a path to approach the Real, God the Exalted. This path requires courtesy, that is, the good manners of the spiritual wayfarer, which is the subject of the second treatise contained here. It is called *The Treatise on the Good Manners of the Spiritual Disciple's Wayfaring*.

Good Manners was dictated by the Imām in 1071 AH, by which time, despite his young age, he was a recognized spiritual master. The treatise was dictated as a reply to a request by one of his early companions for guidelines on how to follow the path.

Translator's Introduction

Manners are important to spiritual growth. It was God Himself who taught the Companions how to behave towards their spiritual master, the Prophet ﷺ, with utmost respect and reverence:

> O you who believe, do not be forward in the presence of God and His Messenger. And fear God. Indeed, God is hearing, knowing. O you who believe, do not raise your voices above the Prophet's voice, nor shout when speaking to him as you shout one to another, lest your works be rendered void without you knowing it. Those who subdue their voices in the presence of the Messenger of God are those whose hearts God had tested for taqwā. For them is forgiveness and a great reward. (QURAN, 49:1-3)

Taqwā is presented in this passage as the foundation of good manners and proper comportment that is becoming of a person who believes in God, the Messenger ﷺ, and the Hereafter. But before learning about good manners, one ought to give some thought to what are bad manners and their characteristics.

It is bad manners of the most sever degree to be informed that the Hereafter is immensely better than this world and is everlasting, yet prefer this world and concentrate all one's energy therein. It is bad manners to be informed that it is possible to draw near to God, yet decide that the effort required to do so is too troublesome and so settle for the minimum necessary to barely escape the Fire. It is bad manners to be informed that some people ascertain profound knowledge of God through contemplation, yet decide that other things are more important as the objects of your concerns. It is bad manners to devote time and energy to studying the insignificant and the ephemeral, yet neglect to devote equal time (at least) in studying that which helps deliver one from chastisement in the Hereafter and from moral indifference in this life. The Prophet ﷺ said, "God loathes those who are learnéd of the affairs of this world but are ignorant of the Hereafter." For it behooves those who have been gifted by God with intelligence and skills to apply these gifts toward what benefits them in the most profound way, to gain knowledge and insight about the Real and the purpose He has created us. This is not to say that one should abandon the world altogether; on the contrary, Islam encourages excellence in things of this world, but not at the expense of matters related to the Hereafter and religious conduct of one's life. Detachment from the world is a thing of the heart, a mental attitude, an objective view of prioritization, so that one does everything that is required to do, but without inordinate preoccupation. As for studying the sciences of religion, it is a duty that no Muslim can evade. "Seeking knowledge is an obligation upon every Muslim man and woman," said the Prophet ﷺ. This goes side by side with learning a trade, a craft, or obtaining higher university degrees.

As for the good manners of spiritual wayfaring, they are meant to shape one's attitudes and behavior towards God the Creator. Next come good manners with the Prophet ﷺ, his Companions, and family; then the shaykh or spiritual master, other teachers, and other men of God; then with the brothers on the path, other Muslims, and finally with creation at large. For there are good manners to be observed with all humanity as well as the creatures of the earth.

Learning spiritual courtesy with one's brothers and fellow Muslims lends to one's learning of spiritual courtesy with the shaykh. This in turn will lead to learning spiritual courtesy with the Prophet ﷺ, which will lead to the ultimate goal of mastering the kind of conduct necessary if one is to be accepted by God, Exalted and Majestic is He. However, in practice, all these have to be implemented simultaneously. The result to be expected appears at each level only when the previous level has been sufficiently mastered.

The Treatise on the Good Manners of the Spiritual Disciple's Wayfaring[2] was conceived in such a manner as to be profitable to all wayfarers, given that it is a manual of behavior that is entirely based on the Quran and *Sunna*, the theoretical knowledge of the

Translator's Introduction

Imām, as well as his personal experience. It is priceless in that, as mentioned above, it is not addressed to the affiliates of a particular path and is capable of being assimilated with ease and implemented without need for clarifications from a master; and it was written in accordance with the dictates of our time. No shaykh will disagree with its contents or say that in his particular path they do things differently. On the contrary, all will agree that this pattern of behavior must constitute the common denominator to which all *tarīqa*-specific practices may subsequently be added.

Imām al-Ḥaddād once said, "The path's outward [dimension] is knowledge; its inward is understanding; its yield is a secret; and its ultimate end is to lose oneself in God." This work has to do with the first two of these four.

The English version of this treatise was first published in Britain in the early 1980's in a limited edition. The text has been thoroughly revised for this edition. We have omitted some of the poetry in the first treatise because of the difficulty of rendering it in English both accurately and retaining a taste of the original. As with all other translations of the Imām's works, the chapter numeration and titles are ours.

We ask God to forgive the flaws in our work, grant us sincerity in speech and action, and make it easy for us to enjoy the honor of gathering with the Messenger of God ﷺ, his Companions, family, our teachers, and all other men of God in the abode of serenity and eternal light. *Āmīn!*

Mostafa al-Badawi

MUTUAL REMINDING

*The Treatise of Mutual Reminding
Among Loving Brothers, People of Goodness and Religion*

PROLOGUE

In the name of God, the All-Merciful, the Compassionate

"Transcendent are You! We have no knowledge save that which You have taught us; You are the Knowing, the Wise" (QURAN, 2:32).

All praise belongs to God, Lord of the Worlds, who created man from clay, then made his progeny from an extraction of mean fluid. He rescued the believers who enjoin truth and patience among one another from among those who are in utter loss—excluding them after attributing failure to all of humanity [who do not believe].[3] He commanded His believing servants to assist each other in benevolence and Godfearingness[4] and informed them that the most honorable of them in His sight are those who fear Him most,[5] that He is the Protector of the God-fearing,[6] and that He created *jinn* and humankind for nothing other than to worship Him[7]—not to make their worldly affairs prosper and to amass wealth. On the contrary, He warned them against that through His Trustworthy Prophet ﷺ, who said, "It was not revealed to me, 'Amass money and be a merchant!' Rather, 'Extol the praises of your Lord, be of those who prostrate themselves, and worship your Lord until what is certain comes to you!'"[8]

Therefore, the true happiness and perfection of each person is rooted in obedience with regard to the [Divine] command and that for which humanity was created. One has to immerse oneself in this and devote oneself to it by severing everything that holds back or thwarts one from it, whether they are deviations of deceived fools or the absurdities of the dull and indolent.

May God's blessings be upon our master Muḥammad—the

Master of all the Messengers and the Seal of all the Prophets, whom God sent as a mercy to the worlds—and upon his family, Companions, and those who follow them with excellence until the Day of Judgment.

Now, to proceed.

That which comprehends all goodness and serves as its foundation is *taqwā* in private and in public, secretly and openly. *Taqwā* [the fear of God] is the attribute which gathers for its possessor the good of this world and the next. Because of its importance in religion and its great worth in the eyes of the learnéd, scholars begin their sermons exhorting people to *taqwā*, and include it in their counsels. Because it comprehends all good, it suffices as the obligatory counsel that must be included in the Friday Prayer Sermon [*Khuṭba*].[9] Often, great men of God, when people request formal counsel from them, confine their counsel to enjoining upon them the fear of God.

Taqwā is also the counsel of God, the Lord of the Worlds, to the first and the last of His servants. God the Exalted has said, *We have counseled those who were given the Book before you and [We counsel] you to fear God* (QURAN, 4:131). God the Exalted says, *O people! Fear your Lord who created you of a single soul* (QURAN, 4:1); *O you who believe! Fear God and speak straight words* (QURAN, 33:70); *O you who believe! Fear God as He should be feared* (QURAN, 3:102); *So fear God as much as you can!* (QURAN, 64:16). This means to do everything that is possible in this respect, for *God does not charge a person with more than what He has given him* (QURAN, 65:7). There are many more verses enjoining the fear of God.

The good of both this world and the next were promised by God to those who fear Him. Examples of this are:

> Relief from hardship and bestowal of provision from whence he does not expect: God the Exalted says, *He who fears God, He will make a way out for him and provide him from where he*

does not expect (QURAN, 65:2-3).

Right guidance: God the Exalted says, *This is the Book, no doubt, containing right guidance for the God-fearing* (QURAN, 2:2).

Knowledge: God the Exalted says, *Fear God and God will teach you* (QURAN, 2:282).

Discernment, expiation of bad actions, and forgiveness of sins: God, Transcendent and Exalted, says, *If you fear God, He will give you discernment, expiate your bad actions, and forgive you* (QURAN, 8:29). Certain commentators have stated that *discernment* is a guidance in the heart which discriminates between truth and falsehood.

Protection: God the Exalted says, *God is the Protector of the God-fearing* (QURAN, 45:19).

Being with God: God the Exalted says, *Know that God is with the God-fearing* (QURAN, 2:194). This means that God is with His support, succor, and protection.

Salvation and deliverance: God the Exalted says, *Then We shall deliver those who are God-fearing* (QURAN, 19:72).

The promise of Paradise: God says—and August is the Speaker—*The likeness of the Garden that the God-fearing are promised is such that rivers will be flowing in it, of unpolluted water, and rivers of milk of unchanged taste, and rivers of wine delicious to the drinkers, and of honey, clear and pure* (QURAN, 47:15); and [He said], *The garden shall be brought near for the God-fearing, not afar* (QURAN, 50:31).

There are other beautiful and good things, immense favors and generous gifts promised to the God-fearing. It is sufficient honor with regard to *taqwā* that God the Exalted mentions it more than ninety times in His Book. As for enjoining *taqwā* and its merits, the Messenger of God ﷺ said:

> Fear God wherever you are; follow a bad deed with a good one and it shall erase it; and behave toward people in a gracious manner.
>
> I enjoin upon you the fear of God and to hear and obey, even

if you are given a slave for a ruler.

Fear God, even with half a date, if you possess not even that, then with a gracious word.

O God, I ask of You guidance, Godfearingness, continence, and freedom from needs!

There is no superiority for a white man over a black man, nor for an Arab over a non-Arab, except the fear of God. You are all from Adam and Adam is from dust!

[The most honorable of people] are those who fear God most.

Eat only the food of those who fear God, and let only those who fear God eat your food!

'Ā'isha, may God be pleased with her, said, "Nothing of this world was pleasing to the Messenger of God, and no person was pleasing to him save one who feared God."

'Alī, may God honor his countenance, said, "The crops of a people never perish in the presence of the fear of God."

Qatāda said, "It is written in the Torah: 'Fear God, then die wherever you wish!'" Al-A'mash said, "He whose capital is the fear of God, tongues grow weary in describing his profits." Bishr al-Ḥāfī used to recite, "The death of the God-fearing is endless life. / Some have died but are still among the living."

The merits of *taqwā* and of those who possess it are beyond enumeration. Imām al-Ghazālī has composed quite a lengthy exposition of this in his treatise *Minhāj al-'Ābidīn*, and what we just quoted is, in fact, extracted from his work.

ONE

The Meaning of Taqwā

Imām al-Ghazālī has said, "*Taqwā* in the Quran has three meanings. First is *fear* and a sense of *awe*. The second includes obedience and worship. Third is freeing the heart from sins, which is the reality and essence of *taqwā*. In summary, *taqwā* is to guard oneself against the anger of God and His punishment by fulfilling His commandments and abstaining from what He has made prohibited. The reality of *taqwā* is that your Lord never sees you where He has forbidden you to be, nor does He miss you where He has commanded you to be.[10] May peace be upon you.

TWO
The Recompense of Works

Those possessed of sound hearts and upright minds know that they will be requited for what they do in this life, that they will reap what they sow, that they will be judged just as they judge others, and that they are heading toward that which they have forwarded for themselves. How can such people not know this or fail to be certain of this when what they believe and trust in comes from what they hear in the perfect revelation of God and the utterances of His Prophet ﷺ? They are sources that impart conviction and certitude in one whose heart God illuminates and whose breast He dilates. So be present of heart and attentive of ear and listen to what may awaken you from your heedlessness and rouse you from your slumber. Act well for your own good, and save yourself *"on a day when no wealth shall avail, nor children, save those who come to God with a sound heart"* (QURAN, 26:88-89).

God the Exalted says, *To God belongs what is in the heavens and what is in the earth, that He may recompense those who have done wrong with their doings and recompense those who have done good with good* (QURAN, 53:31). And He says, Exalted is He, *And there is nothing for man except what he has striven for, and his strivings shall surely be seen; then he will be recompensed for it to the full, and to your Lord is the final end* (QURAN, 53:39-42). And He says, Exalted is He, *It is not by your wishes, nor the wishes of* the People of the Book. *He who does wrong will be recompensed accordingly, and he will find neither protector nor ally other than God. And he who does good, whether he be male or female, and he is a believer, such will enter the Garden, and they will not be wronged [so much as] the thread of a date-stone* (QURAN, 4:123-24). And He says, Exalted is He, *He who does an atom's weight of good will see it, and he who does an atom's weight of evil will see it* (QURAN, 99:7-8). And He says, Exalted is He, *God charges no soul except that which it can bear. It will be requited for whatever good and whatever evil it has earned* (QURAN, 2:286). And He says, Exalted is He, *He who does good, it is for his own self, and he who does wrong it is against it; and your Lord is not unjust to His servants* (QURAN, 41:46). And He says, Exalted is He, *[Judgment Day shall be] a day when each soul will find the good it has done brought near; as for the evil it has done, it will wish that there would be a mighty distance between them. God warns you to beware of Him, and God is kind to the servants* (QURAN, 3:30). And He says, Exalted is He, *Fear a day when you shall be returned to God, then each soul shall be recompensed for what it has earned, and they shall not be wronged* (QURAN, 2:281). It is said that this verse was the last verse of the Quran to be revealed.

The Messenger of God ﷺ said, "The Holy Spirit whispered into my heart: Live as long as you wish, you shall die! Love whatever you wish, you shall be separated from it! Do whatever you wish, you shall be rewarded for it!" And the Prophet ﷺ said, "Benevolence does not decay, sins are not forgotten, the Judge does not die. As you judge, so shall you be judged." And he relates on behalf of his Lord, "O My servants, it is but your deeds that I count for you, then I shall pay you in full for them. He who then finds good, let him thank God and he who finds otherwise, let him blame none but himself." And he said, "Do not insult the dead, for they have gone to that which they had forwarded [for themselves]." And he said, "A slave may be raised to a higher rank in the Garden than his master. The master will say, 'O Lord! This man was my slave in the world!' He will say, Transcendent is He, 'I have merely rewarded him for his deeds.'"

ʿAlī, may God honor his countenance, said, "This world is the abode of works; there are no rewards in it. The Hereafter is the abode of rewards, there are no works in it. So act in the abode of no rewards for the sake of the abode of no works!"

Al-Ḥasan al-Baṣrī, may God have mercy on him, said, "God will say to the people of the Garden, 'Enter the Garden through mercy, dwell therein perpetually by your good intentions, and take your shares of it by your works!'"

All the aforementioned quotes that indicate the occurrence of recompense were provided as a reminder; otherwise they are well known to common believers and the elite alike. They are so well known that even the most simpleminded of believers are privy to them.

THREE

God's Satisfaction and His Wrath

It was God's will to associate His good pleasure to obedience to Him, and His wrath to disobedience. He promised those who obey Him admittance into the Garden by His mercy and those who disobey Him to be cast into the Fire according to His justice and wisdom. God the Exalted has said:

> These are the bounds of God. He who obeys God and His Messenger, He will admit him to gardens beneath which rivers flow, abiding therein forever. That is the immense triumph. And he who disobeys God and His Messenger, and transgresses His bounds, He will admit him into a fire, abiding therein forever, and his will be a humiliating torment. (QURAN, 4:13-14)

He has commanded His believing servants to hasten to His forgiveness and His Garden, and to protect themselves and their families from the Fire, by conforming to His commands and avoiding disobedience. God has said, *Hasten to forgiveness from your Lord and a garden the breadth of which is the heavens and earth, prepared for the God-fearing* (QURAN, 3:133). And God the Exalted says, *O you who believe, protect yourselves and your families from a fire, the fuel of which is people and stones. Upon it are angels, severe and powerful, who do not disobey God in what He commands them and do as they are commanded!* (QURAN, 66:6).

FOUR
The Reward of the Pious

God the Exalted says, *He who does good, whether he be male or female, and is a believer, We shall cause him to live a good life* (QURAN, 16:97). And, *God has promised those of you who believe and do good works that He shall cause them to rule in the land, as He caused those before them to rule, that he shall establish firmly for them their religion, which He has chosen for them, and that He shall change their fear into security* (QURAN, 24:55). And He says, Exalted is He, *Those who believe and do good works, We shall not waste the reward of those who do excellent works. They shall have Gardens of Eden, beneath which rivers flow. Therein they shall be adorned with bracelets of gold, wearing green clothes of silk and brocade, leaning therein upon couches. How fair the reward and how excellent the resting place!"* (QURAN, 18:30-31). And [God] says, Exalted is He, *Those who believe and do good works, the All-Merciful shall give them affection* (QURAN, 19:96). Ibn ʿAbbās, may God be pleased with him, said about this last passage, "He will love them and cause the believers to love them also."

The Messenger of God ﷺ said, "God the Exalted says, 'He who shows hostility to a *walī* of Mine,[11] on him I declare war! My servant draws nearer to Me with nothing I love more than that which I have made incumbent upon him. And My servant ceases not to draw nearer to me with supererogatory devotions until I love him. Once I love him, I become his hearing with which he hears, his eyesight with which he sees, his hand with which he strikes, and his foot on which he walks. Should he ask of Me, I shall give him, and should he seek My protection, I shall protect him.'"

Therefore, he who does what is obligatory upon him, then adds supererogatory acts of devotion in abundance in order to draw nearer to God, God honors him with this great love which renders his every movement by God and for God.

The Messenger ﷺ also relates from God the Exalted, "When My servant draws nearer to Me by a handspan, I draw nearer to him an armspan. When he draws nearer to Me an armspan, I draw nearer to him two armspans. When he comes to Me walking, I come to him running." The servant draws nearer to his Lord by obeying and serving Him. The Lord draws nearer to His servant by His favor and mercy.

The Messenger ﷺ relates as well from God the Exalted, "I have prepared for My virtuous servants [in Paradise] that which no eye has seen, no ear has heard, and no human heart has ever imagined."

In the Psalms it is said, "O Son of Adam! Obey Me and I shall fill your heart with independence, your two hands with provision, and your body with health."

And God said to the world, "O world! He who serves Me, serve him, but he who serves you, make him your servant!"

Bishr ibn al-Ḥārith, may God's mercy be upon him, said, "People of goodness possess both this world and the next."

And Yaḥyā ibn Muʿādh has said, "Sons of this world are served by slaves, but sons of the Hereafter are served by free men."

O my brother, if you wish to have rank that does not vanish, eminence that does not diminish, honor that is permanent, and glory that is perpetual, then obey your Lord! For God has placed all these—[rank, eminence, honor, and glory]—in His obedience. He graciously bestows these things on those of His servants who obey Him. He has honored servants who obeyed Him by freeing them from servitude to their whims and appetites, purifying their hearts from the impurity of attending to things ephemeral; wrought at their hands supernatural events and wondrous miracles, such as knowledge of the unseen, the abundance of *baraka*, and the answering of prayers. Thereafter, people took of their lights, followed in their footsteps, implored God to relieve their own hardships for their sake, requested Him by their rank with Him to protect them from harm, beseeched Him by their footprints to fulfill their requests, and sought the *baraka* of the dust of their tombs. But God gave them more than that; He cast of His light into their hearts, filled them with the purest of His knowledge and love, comforted them in their retreats with the remembrance of Him, so that they felt estranged from His creation, prepared for them permanent bliss in the Abode of Bliss, and promised them to see His Noble Countenance—and greater still will be His satisfaction with them.

That is the great triumph! (QURAN, 44:57). *For the like of this let workers work!* (QURAN, 37:61).

FIVE
The Abasement of the Corrupt

God the Exalted says, *He who comes to his Lord as a criminal, his shall be Hell, in which he will neither die nor live* (QURAN, 20:74). And He says, Exalted is He, *Or do those who commit sins think they will outstrip Us? Evil is their judgment* (QURAN, 29:4). The meaning of "outstrip" here is to evade and stand out of reach [of God]. And God the Exalted says, *He who disobeys God and His Messenger, he has erred into manifest error* (QURAN, 33:36). The

Messenger of God ﷺ said, "He who commits adultery is not a believer while he commits adultery, and he who steals is not a believer while he steals, and he who drinks alcohol is not a believer while he drinks." And he said ﷺ, "When the servant sins, it becomes a black spot in his heart. Should he repent, his heart becomes clear again. But if he repeats it, the black spot will enlarge until the [whole] heart turns black." This is His saying, Exalted is He, *No, but what they have wrought has covered over their hearts* (QURAN, 83:14). The Messenger ﷺ said, "Hardness of the heart comes from frequent sins." He said moreover ﷺ, "The servant's provision may be withheld because of a sin he committed."

And God revealed to Moses ﷺ, "O Moses! The first of my creation to die was Satan, for he was the first to disobey Me; and he who disobeys Me, I consider him dead."

Saʿīd ibn al-Musayyab, may God's mercy be on him, said, "People honor themselves with nothing [better] than obedience to God, nor do they debase themselves with [anything worse than] disobedience to God. It is sufficient support from God to the believer for one to see his enemy disobeying God."

Muḥammad ibn Wāsiʿ said, "Sins in succession slay the heart."

One of the virtuous predecessors has said, "If you disobey God, knowing that He sees you, you are scorning God's vision, but if you disobey Him, thinking that He does not see you, you are a disbeliever."

Wahāb ibn Ward, may God's mercy be upon him, was asked, "Does he who disobeys God find pleasure in worship?" He answered, "No! Neither does he who [merely] *intends* disobedience." The virtuous predecessors used to say, "Sins are the harbinger of disbelief."

In summary, continually indulging into sin is a sign of having fallen in the sight of God and deserving of His displeasure. He who persists in this is detestable to the All-Merciful; he is the Devil's ally and the believers' object of disgust.[12] So beware, my brother, of exposing yourself to God's displeasure and chastisement by disobeying Him. Should your soul incite you to sin, remind it of God's absolute awareness and sight of you. Place fear into it by recalling God's warnings of the painful torment and formidable punishment that awaits those who disobey Him. Had it been that the punishment for committing sins was merely being debarred from reaching the rank of the *foremost* [*al-sābiqūn*] or being deprived of the reward of those most excellent in deeds [*al-muḥsinīn*], this alone would have been sufficient [deterrence]. What, then, when indulgence in sin leads to shame, Hellfire, and the wrath and displeasure of the Compeller, before which the heavens and earth cannot stand? We ask God for safety, by His grace.

SIX
Delight in Obedience

The Messenger of God ﷺ said, "He who is pleased by his good deeds and displeased by his evil ones is a believer." O believer, when God grants you the good fortune of acting in His obedience, let your joy be great; thank God in abundance for honoring you with His service and choosing you to attend to Him; and ask Him to accept, by His grace, whatever He has made easy for you in the way of virtuous behavior. ʿAlī, may God honor his countenance, said, "Be more anxious for your works to be accepted than for them to be done, for no accepted deed is small."[13]

Always acknowledge your shortcomings in fulfilling your duties to your Lord, even when you are most determined and energetic in His obedience, for His rights upon you are immense: He created you from nothing; His favors overflow upon you; He treats you with His grace and generosity; you obey Him by His power and His ability; and you worship Him by His help and mercy.

Beware of soiling the robe of your faith and blackening the

countenance of your heart by committing that which your Lord has forbidden you. Should you fall into sin, even if it is infrequent, hasten to repent, return to obedience, feel remorse, and ask forgiveness in abundance. Remain fearful and apprehensive, for the believer remains fearful and apprehensive to the extreme even when he is sincere in his obedience and service. You already know how the prophets behaved, even though they were inerrant, and the saints, even though they are guarded. They were fearful and wary, though their works were good and their sins rare or non-existent. You are more worthy of this [fear and anxiety] than they, for they were better acquainted than you with the immensity of God's mercy, better thinking than you of God, more truthful than you in hoping for His pardon, and more hopeful than you in His generosity and grace. Follow in their footsteps and you will be safe and secure. Follow their path and you will attain to success and many profits. Seek protection in God, for he who seeks protection in God has been guided to a straight path.

SEVEN
The Four Obstacles to Obedience

Because the abode of this world is founded on hardship and trial, kneaded with trouble and distress, and filled with preoccupations and distractions, the things that divert one away from acts of obedience abound, as are those things that incite to transgression. These distractions are numerous, but may be reduced to four categories: The first is *ignorance*, the second *weakness of faith*, the third *long hopes*, and the fourth *eating illicit or dubious food*.[14] We shall briefly discuss each of these four, God willing, to demonstrate how blameworthy they truly are and to show how to guard oneself and free oneself from them. Success is from God.

EIGHT
Ignorance

As for ignorance, it is the origin of all evil, the root of every harm. Ignorant folk are included in the Prophet's saying ﷺ, "The world is accursed, and accursed is what is in it, except the remembrance of God and the learnéd and those learning." It is said that when God created ignorance He said to it, "Come!" but it moved away. He said to it, "Go!" but it came. Then He said, "By My might, I have created nothing in creation more hateful to Me than you, and I shall place you amongst the worst of my creation!" ʿAlī, may God honor his countenance, said, "There is no enemy worse than ignorance. A man is the enemy of that which he has no knowledge of."

Ignorance is blameworthy according to both textual and rational proof, and its [harm] is hardly unknown to anyone. An ignorant man succumbs to neglecting obligations and committing sins, whether he wishes it or not, because one who is ignorant neither knows the obligations God has enjoined upon him nor the misdeeds God has forbidden. A person can leave the shadows of ignorance only by the light of knowledge.

How excellent are the words of Shaykh ʿAlī ibn Abī Bakr when he said, "Ignorance is a fire that burns a man's religion. / And its extinguishing water is knowledge."

So you must learn what God has made incumbent for you to learn. You are not obliged to acquire extensive knowledge, but that without which your faith remains unsound you must learn. Examples of these are the proper performance of your obligatory rites of worship and how to avoid what is prohibited. This is an immediate duty with regard to immediate [obligations], and for those matters that may be deferred, it is a deferred duty. Mālik ibn Dīnār, may God have mercy on him, used to say, "He who seeks knowledge for himself, a little will suffice him; but he who seeks knowledge for the people, the people's needs are numerous."

NINE
Weakness of Faith

Weakness of faith is an awful affliction from which many blameworthy things arise, like neglecting to act on what one knows, disregarding the enjoining of good and forbidding of evil, harboring hopes for forgiveness without striving for it, worrying about provision, fearing people, and other unfortunate character traits. A person's observance of God's commands and prohibitions is only proportionate to the strength of his faith. The most obvious proof of a person's weakness in faith is his neglect of injunctions and committing of contraventions.

Every believer should strive to strengthen his faith, and there are three wayss do so:

The first is to listen [mindfully] to the verses of the Quran and the statements of the Prophet ﷺ that reveal the promises [of Paradise], threats [of Hell], tidings of the Hereafter, the stories of the Prophets, what miracles they were confirmed with, what happened to their opponents, the detachment from the world and the [ardent] desire for the Hereafter which the virtuous predecessors possessed, and other things handed down. The second is to observe and ponder the kingdom of the heavens and the earth and what wondrous signs and beautiful creatures they contain. The third is to persevere in acts of goodness and to guard oneself from falling into sin and contravention, for faith is both words and deeds. It increases with obedience and diminishes with sins. All these that we have just mentioned increase faith and strengthen certitude. And God is the Helper.

TEN
Long Hopes

Long hopes are extremely blameworthy. They lead one to work for prosperity of his worldly life at the expense of ruining his Hereafter. The Messenger of God ﷺ, "The first folk among this nation will be saved by detachment from this world and short hopes, while the last will perish by greed for this world and long hopes." And he said ﷺ, "Four things are of wretchedness: dry eyes, hardness of the heart, greed, and long hopes." The Prophet ﷺ prayed, "I seek Your protection from every hope that may distract me!"

ʿAlī, may God honor his countenance, said, "What I fear most for you is that you follow your passions and have long hopes. Following passions repels from the truth; and having long hopes causes you to forget the Hereafter."

It is a maxim that he whose hopes are long, his works are bad. [To harbor] long hopes is to feel secure that you will remain in this world for a very long time. It shows an excessive foolishness and extreme stupidity, for long hopes push away certitude [about death] and [attracts] attachment to the illusion [of a perpetual life]. If you say to such a person in the evening, "Are you certain you will live until morning?" or if you say to him in the morning, "Are you certain you will live until evening?" he will say: "No!" Still, he works for this world as if he is never to die, to the point that should he be told that he will remain in this world forever, he will be incapable of adding more desire and greed for it. What can be more foolish than that?

Furthermore, long hopes are at the root of a number of evil character traits and acts which hinder obedience [of God's commands] and invite to sin. Examples of this are avidity, avarice, and the fear of poverty. Among the worst are finding comfort in this world, working to improve one's lot in it, and striving to amass its debris.[15] He has said, may blessings and peace be upon him, "I was sent for the ruin of this world, he who makes it prosper is not of me."[16]

Long hopes bring about procrastination, which is a most sterile thing, for it never gives birth to anything good. It is said that most of the woeful howling of the people of the Fire is due to [their] procrastination. For he who procrastinates is ever lazy in obedience, slow in repentance, until death overtakes him, then he will say: *"O Lord! Were You to only reprieve me for a short time, that I may give charity and be one of the righteous"* (QURAN, 63:10). But it will be said to him: *"God will not delay a soul whose time has come"* (QURAN, 63:11). *Did We not give you lives long enough that he who reflects may indeed reflect, and the warner came to you? So taste! For the unjust have no helper* (QURAN, 35:37). The procrastinator leaves this world with endless sorrow and limitless regret.

O my brother, shorten your hopes, and let your time stand before your eyes and your hope behind your back. Seek help in this by remembering the "defeater of pleasures" in abundance, the "disperser of companies."[17] Reflect on those who have preceded you, relatives and acquaintances [who have passed on]. Bring to mind just how near death is, for it is the nearest thing lying in wait. Be ready for it; expect its pouncing upon you any time.

The Messenger of God ﷺ used to say, "By He in whose Hand is my soul, I never raised my eyes thinking I would lower them before my soul is taken, nor have I ever eaten a morsel thinking that I would swallow it without choking on it because of death." Sometimes he rubbed the wall for *tayammum*, and, when it was said to him, "Water is near," he replied, "How do I know that I will ever reach it.?"

Al-Ṣiddīq, may God be pleased with him, used to recite, "Every man wakes up in his home / with death nearer to him than the laces of his sandals."

The Proof of Islam, may God have mercy on him, wrote,

"Know that death does not pounce at a specific time, situation, or age, but it is certain to pounce. Therefore, preparing for it has priority over preparing for this world."

ELEVEN
Illicit and Suspect Food

Consuming illicit and doubtful food inevitably hinders obedience and invites to transgression. The Messenger of God ﷺ is reported to have said, "He who eats *ḥalāl* [permissible], his members obey, whether he wishes it or not; but he who eats *ḥarām* [forbidden food], his members sin, whether he wishes it or not." And, "Eat what you will, for that is how you will act." And a certain Gnostic once said, "People are severed from the truth and excluded from the circle of sainthood only because they do not scrutinize what they eat."

He whose food is illicit or suspect, even when he acts in obedience, his acts are unacceptable to God, for God the Exalted says, *"God only accepts [deeds] from those who fear Him"* (QURAN, 5:27). God is good and accepts only what is good.[18]

O my brother, refrain from eating the illicit, for this is obligatory, and the suspect, for this is dictated by scrupulousness. And seek only the licit, for this is an obligation among the other obligations. When you obtain licit food and clothes, eat with moderation and dress with moderation. Do not be excessive, for the licit does not bear excessiveness. Beware of eating to satiety, for eating licit food to satiety is the beginning of evil. (What then of illicit food?) The Messenger ﷺ has said, "The Son of Adam never fills a vessel worse than his stomach. It should suffice the Son of Adam a few morsels to keep his back straight. If he must, then a third [of his stomach] for his food, a third for his beverage, and a third for his breath."

TWELVE
Sincerity

God the Exalted says, *I created jinn and mankind only that they may worship Me* (QURAN, 51:56). And, *O My servants who believe, My earth is vast. It is I whom you should worship* (QURAN, 29:56).

O believer, may God grant you success, you must free yourself for the worship of your Lord by removing all hindrances and avoiding all diversions and obstacles. Know that worship cannot be sound without knowledge, and knowledge and works cannot be of benefit without sincerity, for it is the axis around which everything revolves, the foundation upon which everything stands. As Abū al-Qāsim al-Qushayrī said, may God's mercy be upon him, "Sincerity is to have no other intention than the Real in your acts of obedience. Which means that you should intend, with your acts of obedience, to draw nearer to God, nothing else; no ostentation before a created being, wish to be praised among people, [wish] of their owing you a favor, or anything other than drawing nearer to God." He said, "It would be true to say that sincerity is to free the act from watching created beings." This is the essence of this chapter.

THIRTEEN
Ostentation

Beware of ostentation,[19] for it invalidates what you do, leads to the loss of reward [for your deeds], and brings on detestation and punishment. The Messenger of God ﷺ called it the "lesser idolatry."[20] An authentic tradition says, "The first of God's creation to fuel the Fire will be three: A man who recites the Quran so that it is said, 'He is a reciter"; a man who is killed, having fought only so it is said, 'He is courageous'; and a wealthy man who gives charity only so it is said, 'He is generous.'"

Ostentation is to seek importance in people's eyes with acts that draw nearer to God, such as ritual Prayers and Fasts. Should you perceive ostentation in yourself, do not try to rid yourself of it by abandoning works, thus pleasing the Devil. Works that can only be done in public, such as going on Pilgrimage, *jihād*, acquiring knowledge, congregational Prayers, and similar things, you should perform publicly as God has commanded you. Strive against your ego and seek God's help! As for other kinds of works, like Fasting, night vigils, charity, and [Quran] recitation, these you should go to extremes to conceal, for performing them in secret is unreservedly preferable, except for those who are safe from ostentation, who hope to be emulated by others, and who are qualified for this.

FOURTEEN
Conceit

Beware of conceit, for it invalidates works. The Messenger of God ﷺ said, "Conceit eats good works just as fire eats firewood." And he said, "Three things are ruinous: avarice that one obeys, passion that one follows, and admiration that one has for himself." Conceit is for someone to see himself as important and his behavior as excellent. From this arises showing off one's works, feeling superior to others, and being self-satisfied. As Ibn ʿAṭāʾillāh said, may God's mercy be upon him, "The root of every sin, distraction, or lust is self-satisfaction." He who is satisfied with himself does not see his shortcomings. And he who is unaware of his shortcomings, how can he succeed?

FIFTEEN
Love of This World

The Messenger of God ﷺ said, "The love of this world is the head of every sin." Moreover, it is at the root of every affliction, the origin of every calamity, the essence of every temptation, and the source of every hardship. Its evil has spread in these times and has become a grave danger, involving everyone. It is exhibited shamelessly as if it were not disgraceful and reprehensible. It has taken over the hearts of people and resulted in their excessive eagerness to work for the world and accumulate its debris. They roam about with their nets, fishing for suspect and illegal wares, as if God had made affluence in this world an obligation, just like Prayer and Fasting.

For this reason religion is losing its landmarks: the lights of certitude are being extinguished, the tongues of the reminders are silent; the paths of guidance have disappeared; and the paths of ruin are increasingly treaded. By God! This is the blind and deaf temptation, dark and black; where no prayer is answered and no caller heard. The Master of all Prophets ﷺ spoke truly when he said, "Each nation has its temptation, and that of my nation is money. Each nation has its calf, the calf of my nation is the *dīnār* and the *dirham*." In other words, each nation has something particular to which it inordinately attends to that leads to neglecting the worship of God, just as the Children of Israel attended to the worship of the [golden] calf, abandoning the worship of God, Exalted is He. And God knows best.

CONCLUSION

It is good to conclude this brief exposition with a few quotations telling of the fault of [the inordinate love of] this world and of one who makes it his priority. But we must precede this with a rule that can be acted upon and referred back to. And so we say, (and success is from God):

This world[21] is of three kinds: one leading to reward; another leading to being asked to account; and a third leading to torment.

As for that [life] leading to reward, it is one in which you work for and attain good and also escape evil. The world is the riding mount of the believer and the tilling ground of the Hereafter. This consists of the necessities that are lawfully acquired.

As for that which leads one to being asked to account, it is the life which neither prevents you from an obligation nor induces you to indulge in transgression. This is the kind of worldly situation which leads to protracted reckoning [in the Hereafter]. It is that of the rich whom the poor will precede into the Garden by half a day, which is five hundred years.

As for that which leads to torment, it is [living a life] that prevents you from your obligations or lures you into transgression. For its owner, this life is provision for the Fire and his path to the abode of ruin. This is what is meant by the statement, "God orders the world to be cast into the Fire. It cries, 'O Lord! My supporters, my followers!' Then He says—Transcendent is He—'Let its supporters and followers join it!' Then they are indeed made to join it."

Know that the pursuers of this world are of three kinds: Some pursue it with the intention of giving to relatives and comforting the poor. Such people are considered to be generous and they will be rewarded, if their acts match their intentions. However, they lack wisdom, for the wise do not seek that whose consequences they do not really know. Let them heed the lesson in the story of Tha'laba, to whom God the Exalted alludes in the verse: *Among them are those who promised God, "Should He give us of His favor we shall surely give charity"* (QURAN, 9:75).[22]

Others yet have nothing but appetites and pleasures in mind. They are likened to cattle, as God the Exalted has said, *Do you think that most of them hear or understand? They are but like cattle; they are even more astray* (QURAN, 25:44).

Others frequently pursue worldly things for the purpose of boast, bragging, and rivalry. These folk are considered illusioned fools or, worse still, the ruined losers: *Each people know their drinking place* (QURAN, 2:60); *and your Lord knows what their breasts hide and what they reveal* (QURAN, 28:69).

O my brother, counsel yourself honestly and do not betray yourself by feigning something you do not really intend. For you will have combined bankruptcy with false pretense and will lose both this world and the next: *This is the manifest loss* (QURAN, 39:15).

Now that the foregoing discussion has been elucidated, let us now move on to the conclusion, which includes verses of the Book of God, traditions from the *sunna* of the Messenger of God ﷺ, and utterances of the sages among men of God. They concern the insignificance of this world, the speed with which it perishes, and the foolishness of those who are deceived by it and trust in it. These passages encourage those who read them and who possess hearts or listen with attentiveness[23] to detach themselves from [desiring this world].

God the Exalted says, and His utterance is *the reality* and His words *the truth*:

> *The likeness of the life of this world is that of water which we send down from the sky, then the plants of the earth mingled with it, from which men and cattle eat. Then when the earth takes on its ornaments and is embellished, and its people think they have power over it, Our command comes down upon it by night or day, and We make it as reaped [wheat] as if it had not flourished the previous day. Thus We make plain Our signs for a people who reflect.* (QURAN, 10:24)

> And He says, Exalted is He: *We have placed all that is in the earth as an ornament for it, that We may try them as to which of them is best in conduct. Then We will surely reduce all that*

is on it to barren dust. (QURAN, 18:7-8)

And He says, Exalted is He: *And do not strain your eyes toward what We have given some of them to enjoy from the splendor of the life of this world, through which We only test them. The provision of your Lord is better and more lasting.* (QURAN, 20:131)

And He says, Exalted is He: *He who seeks the harvest of the Hereafter, We increase his harvest; and he who seeks the harvest of this world, We give him of it here, but in the Hereafter he will have no portion.* (QURAN, 42:20)

And He says, Exalted is He: *Know that the life of this world is but play and diversions and adornment and boasting among you and rivalry regarding wealth and children; just as the likeness of rain, the tillers rejoice over its vegetation, but then it withers and you see it turn yellow, soon becoming stubble. In the Hereafter there is severe torment, and [also] forgiveness from God and [His] good pleasure, whereas the life of this world is but the comfort of the deluded.* (QURAN, 57:20)

And He says, Exalted is He: *As for those who transgress and prefer the life of this world, Hell indeed is the abode.* (QURAN, 79:37-39)

The Messenger of God ﷺ said:

This world is accursed, and accursed is what it is in it, except the remembrance of God, the learnéd, and those learning.

Had this world weighed with God the wing of a gnat, He would not have allowed a disbeliever a sip of its water.

This world is a dirty carcass.

God the Exalted has made what comes out of the Son of Adam the example for this world.

This world compared to the Hereafter is just like one of you dipping his finger in the ocean, looking at what it brings back.

Mutual Reminding

On the Day of Arising, everyone will wish that he had been given nothing of this world except the bare necessity.

A difficult obstacle stands before you, and only those who are lightly laden will cross it. A man asked, "Am I one of the lightly laden, O Messenger of God?" He said, "Are you in possession of your day's provision?" He replied, "Yes!" He asked, "Are you in possession of tomorrow's provision?" He replied "No!" The Messenger of God ﷺ said, "Had you been in possession of tomorrow's provision, you would not have been one of the lightly laden."

This world is fair and green and God has given you mastery over it to see how you will do. So beware of God. And beware of women, for by God, it is not poverty that I fear for you, but I fear that this world will be given to you freely as it was freely given to those before you, that you shall compete for it as those before you did, and that it shall destroy you as it destroyed them.

Among the things I fear for you after me is that which will be given to you from among the beauties of this world, its ornaments and embellishments."

Beware of this world for it is more enchanting than Hārūt and Mārūt.[24]

This world is the prison of the believer and the Garden of the disbeliever.

God keeps the world away from His believing servant, just as a careful shepherd keeps his flock away from dangerous pastures.

A sin that cannot be forgiven: the love of this world.

He who loves his Afterlife slights his world, and he who loves his world slights his Afterlife. Choose that which is permanent over that which is ephemeral!

When this world is bitter, the Hereafter will be sweet; but when this world is sweet, the Hereafter will be bitter.

Those who possess plenty will be those who possess little on the Day of Arising, except for those who do this and this. [The Prophet ﷺ gestured with his hand as one giving away money.]

Some people will be brought on the Day of Arising who have works like the mountains of Tihāma, but these will be turned into scattered dust and they will be ordered into the Fire. They used to pray and fast and keep vigil part of the night, but when something of this world caught their attention, they pounced on it.

What have I to do with this world? The likeness of myself and the world is that of a rider riding on a hot day: he rested under a tree for a while, then departed.

He who wakes up in the morning, secure in his home, healthy in his body, possessing his day's provision, he is as if the whole world had been given to him.

I was sent for the ruin of this world; he who works for its prosperity is not of me.

He whose intention is the Hereafter, God makes him rich in his heart, gathers his affair for him, and the world comes to him subdued. But he whose intention is this world, God places poverty between his eyes, disperses his affair, and still nothing of this world will come to him save that which was written for him.

Be in this world as a stranger or a passerby, and count yourself among the people of the graves.

Renounce this world and God will love you. Renounce what is in people's hands and people will love you.

This world is the abode of he who has no abode and the wealth of he who has no wealth. He who is mindless amasses it; he who has no knowledge grieves for it; he who has no understanding envies others for it; and he who has no certainty rejoices in it.

Mutual Reminding

The love of this world never settles in the heart of a servant without him being afflicted with three things: preoccupation, the pressure of which never relents, poverty that never reaches sufficiency, and hope whose limit is never reached.

This world and the Hereafter are both seekers and sought. He who seeks the Hereafter, the world seeks him until he receives all his provision, but he who seeks this world, the Hereafter seeks him until death grasps him by the throat.

The fortunate is he who prefers that which is permanent and of lasting pleasures over that which is ephemeral and of endless torment. He is the one who gives of what is now in his hand for the sake of where he is going, before leaving it to those who will happily spend it after he has toiled to accumulate and monopolize it.

May the servant of this world be wretched and abased! And if he is pricked may he not be treated!

Renouncing this world relieves both the heart and the body, whereas desire for this world increases anxiety and sorrow. Idleness hardens the heart.

Light when it penetrates into the heart, the latter enlarges for it and expands. They asked, "Is there a sign for this?" He replied, "Shunning the abode of illusion, attending to the abode of immortality, and preparing for death before its occurrence."

God revealed to Moses ﷺ, "O Moses! When I love My servant I hide the world from him, thus do I treat those I love! O Moses! When you see wealth coming, say, 'A sin, the punishment of which has been hastened!' But when you see poverty coming, say, 'Welcome to the inner garment of the virtuous!'"

And God revealed to David ﷺ, "O David! He who prefers the desires of this world over the pleasures of the Hereafter, he has grasped the loose handhold. But he who prefers the desire for the Hereafter over the pleasures of this world, he has grasped the firm handhold that never breaks."

And God revealed to Jesus ﷺ, "O Jesus! Tell the Children of Israel to remember two things from Me: tell them to be content with little of their world for the safety of their religion, just as the people of this world are content with little religion for the safety of their world."

And in a revealed scripture God says, "The least I do to a scholar who finds comfort in this world is to remove the sweetness of communing with Me from his heart."

And it is said that God the Exalted said to the world, "O world! Be bitter for my protégés, be not sweet for them so as not to tempt them."

And ʿAlī [ibn Abī Ṭālib], may God honor his countenance, said:

> The likeness of this world and the Hereafter is that of the east and the west; the nearer you draw to the one, the farther you move from the other. They are like the two wives, when you please the one, you anger the other. And they are like two vessels, one empty and the other full; when you pour into the empty one, the other diminishes accordingly.
>
> I found this world to be six things: That which is eaten, the best tasting is honey, and it is the secretion of an insect; that which is drunk, the best is water, and in this both the righteous and the depraved are equal; that which is smelled, the most fragrant is musk, and it is the blood of an animal; that which is worn, the softest is silk, and it is the weaving of a worm; that which is ridden, the worthiest is the mare, and it is that on whose back men are slain; those which one marries, it is but base fluid in base fluid. It is sufficient for you to know that although the woman adorns herself with the best she has, your desire for her is for the basest she has! [SEE "TRANSLATOR'S APPENDIX ONE."]
>
> Happy are those who renounce the world and desire the Hereafter. They are people who take the ground for a carpet, its dust for a bed, its water for perfume, and make supplica-

tion and the Quran their inner and outer garments. They reject the world according to the pattern of Jesus ﷺ."

In this vein they recited:

> God has astute men who divorce the world and fear temptation. They look at it and realize that it is no homeland for the living. They treat it as a sea, making out of their good works ships.

Saʿīd ibn al-Musayyab, may God have mercy on him, said, "This world is vile and it resembles vile people. The vilest is he who acquires it in a manner he should not have," that is, illicitly.

Al-Ḥasan al-Baṣrī, may God have mercy on him, said:

> Death has exposed this world and left no joy in it for anyone who understands. May God have mercy on a man who wears worn out clothes, eats a crust of bread, keeps low to the ground, weeps for his sins, and perseveres in worship.

> When love of this world enters the heart, fear of the Hereafter exits from it. Beware of worldly distractions, for no servant opens a door of this world without several doors of works for the Hereafter being shut before him.

> Wretched is the Son of Adam, he thinks his money too little but never his works. He rejoices when afflicted in his religion, but grieves when afflicted in his worldly things. This world was founded on ailments and diseases. Suppose you are free of ailments and cured of all disease, can you escape death?

Muḥammad al-Bāqir, may God be pleased with him, said, "What is this world? What can it ever be? Is it anything but a mount you ride, a robe you wear, or a woman you marry?"

Wahb ibn Munabbah, may God have mercy on him, said, "The Garden has eight gates. When people will reach them, the guardians will say, 'By our Lord's might! None shall enter it before those who renounced the world and passionately loved the Garden!'"

Muḥammad ibn Sīrīn said, "Two men quarreled about a piece of land. God said to it, 'Speak to them!' The land then said, 'O wretched ones! A thousand one-eyed men owned me before you, let alone the healthy!'"

Abū Ḥāzim al-Madanī, may God have mercy on him, said:

> There is nothing in this world that will delight you without having something stuck to it that will distress you. This world is a place of tortuosity, not of straightness; of toil, not of joy; of affliction, not of affluence.

> His wife once told him, "Winter is coming, we must have food, clothes, and firewood." He answered, "All these are not inescapable necessities, what is inescapable is that we shall die, then be resurrected, then stand before God, then it will be either the Garden or the Fire."

> You never extend your hand to something of this world without finding that a depraved man has overtaken you to it.

> God's favor in that which He withholds from me of this world is greater than His favor in granting me some of it.

> What has elapsed of the world is a dream, and what remains of it is but hopes.

Luqmān said, "He who sells this world for the next wins both, but he who sells the Hereafter for this world loses both." And he counseled his son thus, "This world is a deep sea where many people have drowned, let your ship on it be the fear of God, fill it with faith, let her sails be reliance, that perhaps you may be saved, and still I think you may not."

Mālik ibn Dīnār said, may God's mercy be on him, "When the body is ill, neither food nor beverage benefits it, nor sleep, nor rest. Similar is the heart, if overcome by the love of this world, it benefits not from counseling." And he said to his companions, "I shall pray, you say Amen! O God! Allow nothing of this world into the house of Mālik, neither little nor much!"

When he went out of his house, he tied the door with a rope, saying, "Were it not for the dogs, I would have left it open."

Once he passed by a man planting a palm shoot. He remained

away for a while then passed by the same place again, the shoot had taken root and produced. He inquired about the man and was told that he had died, so he said:

> He hoped for the world to remain his
> But he who hoped died before his hope
> He planted a shoot and took care of it
> The shoot lived on, the man died

It is said that *Lā ilāha illa'llāh* protects those who say it unless they come to trade their religion for this world, then when they say it, God will say: "You lie! You do not mean it in truth!"

One of our ancestors used to say, "O You who keeps the sky from falling upon the earth, keep this world away from me!"

Ibrāhīm ibn Adham once entered upon [the caliph] al-Manṣūr. The latter asked him, "O Ibrāhīm, what do you have to say? He answered, "We patch up our world by tearing our religion into pieces. / So that neither our religion remains, nor what we are patching."

A man said to Dāwūd al-Ṭā'ī, "Counsel me!" He replied, "Fast from the world and break your fast with the Hereafter, and run away from people as you would from a lion!"

Another man saw him in a dream, running. He asked him, "O Abū Sulaymān, what is with you?" He replied, "Just now I have escaped from prison!" Having awakened, the man was told, "Dāwūd al-Ṭā'ī has died."

Al-Fuḍayl ibn 'Iyāḍ, may God's mercy be upon him, said, "All evil is gathered in a house, the key of which is desire for this world; and all good is gathered in a house, the key of which is renunciation of the world." And he said, "Had the world been made of perishable gold and the Hereafter of permanent clay, we should have preferred permanent clay to perishable gold. What, then, when the world is ephemeral clay and the Hereafter permanent gold?" He said, moreover, "Were this world to be brought to me and were it to be said, 'Take it, licitly, with no reckoning!' I would have protected myself from its filth as one of you protects himself from a carcass he passes lest it soils his clothes.'"

Imām al-Shāfiʿī, may God's mercy be upon him, said, "Were this world to be sold on the market, I would not buy it for a loaf of bread, for the troubles it contains."

Bishr ibn al-Ḥārith, may God's mercy be upon him, said, "He who asks of His Lord this world is asking Him to prolong his standing before Him [on Judgment Day]."

Darrār ibn Damra said, describing ʿAlī, may God honor his countenance:

> He felt estranged from the world and its beauty, and was intimate with night and its darkness. I bear witness that I saw him once when night had fallen, and the stars had risen, wakeful in his retreat, like a man that had been stung, restless as though wounded, weeping sorrowfully, holding his beard, and saying, "O world! Deceive other than myself! Is it for me that you beautify yourself? Is it to me that you manifest yourself? I have divorced you thrice; there can be no return, for your span is short, your worth insignificant, and your danger great! Ah! The scarcity of provision, the length of the way, and the estrangement of traveling!"

One of our ancestors said, "Wretched is the Son of Adam: he is satisfied with an abode of which what is licit leads to reckoning, and what is illicit leads to torment. When he takes it licitly, he is asked to account for its pleasure; if he takes it illicitly he is tormented for it."

Yaḥyā ibn Muʿādh, may God's mercy be on him, said, "Let your gazing at this world be a lesson, your renunciation of it a choice, and your taking from it a necessity." And he said, may God's mercy be on him, "I have abandoned this world because of its excessive troubles, its lack of sufficiency, the speed with which it vanishes, and the resentful envy of the companions it gives you." He also said, "This world is Satan's shop: he who takes anything from it, he follows him until he retrieves it. This world from beginning to end is not worth an hour's grief, how more so with a lifetime of grief and still a small share of it?"

[Caliph Hārūn] al-Rashīd asked for a drink of water and it was brought to him. Ibn al-Sammāk was there. He asked him, "Were you to be prevented from drinking this water, would you buy it with your kingdom?" He said, "Yes!" He said, "Vile is a world that is not worth a drink of water!"

One of the ancients who had lived very long was asked to describe the world. He said, "A house with two doors; I entered through one and exited through the other. I saw years of affliction and years of affluence, newborn babes being born and dying men dying; were it not for the newborn none would remain, were it not for the dead the world would be unable to contain them."

A sage once said, "This world is but ruin; more ruined is the heart of he who works for it. The Hereafter is flourishing, more flourishing is the heart of he who works for it."

Another sage was asked, "Who does this world belong to?" He said, "To he who abandons it." They said, "Who does the Hereafter belong to?" He said "To he who seeks it."

An ascetic was asked, "How do you perceive this world?" He said, "Bodies are being worn out, yet hopes are ever renewed; death is ever approaching and hopes ever receding." They said, "How about its people?" He said, "He who has acquired it is stressed and he who has missed it is distressed."

The Imām [al-Ghazālī], the Proof of Islam, says in the *Iḥyā'*:

> This world is God's enemy, that of His saints, and that of His enemies. As for being God's enemy, it is by obstructing God's servants' path. This is why He has not looked at it since He created it. As for being God's saints' enemy, it is by adorning itself for them, overwhelming them with its beauty and freshness, so that they have to bear the bitterness of patience in resisting it. As for being God's enemies' enemy, it is by luring them with its cunning and stratagems, catching them in its net, so that they trust in it and depend on it. It will let them

down at their time of greatest need, so that what they reap of it is severe grief. Then it will deprive them of happiness forever. They are sorry to leave it, they cry for help against its ruses, but no help is forthcoming, on the contrary, it is said to them: *"Fall back therein and do not speak to Me!"* (QURAN, 23:10). *Those are they who traded the life of this world for the Hereafter, their torment will not be lightened, nor will they be helped* (QURAN, 2:86).

Verses and hadiths concerning this subject are more numerous than to be counted or exhausted. That which we have quoted should be sufficient, a lesson for he who reflects and a reminder for he who remembers: *Only they remember who are repentant* (QURAN, 40:30).

AFTERWORD

We conclude by quoting some of the utterances of the leader of all ascetics, God's proof against them, Jesus son of Mary, may the best of blessings and peace be upon our Prophet Muḥammad and him.

> This world is a bridge, so cross it; do not build on it! O seeker of this world, who wishes to use it righteously, your leaving it is more righteous. The love of this world and that of the Hereafter cannot be united in the believing heart, just as water and fire cannot be united in a single vessel.

> This world is but whatever contingencies are at hand, consumed by both the righteous and the depraved. The Hereafter is a true promise; there judgment belongs to an Able King.

> Do not take this world for a lord, that it may not take you for slaves. Treasure your treasures with He who will not lose them, for worldly treasures are prone to be stricken by calamity. And he whose treasure is with God fears no calamities.

> My food is hunger, my inner garment is fear, my clothing is

wool, my prayer in winter is when the sun rises, my lamp is the moon, my riding mount is my two feet, my food and fruit are what the earth grows. I sleep by night possessing nothing, yet I see none on earth richer than I.

I wonder at he who is forgetful but not forgotten,[25] he who hopes for this world when death is seeking him, and he who builds a palace when the grave is his dwelling. The fear of God and the love of Paradise[26] separate one from the beauties of this world and grant him patience in hardship. Eating barley and sleeping on refuse heaps with the dogs is a small price for Paradise.

O apostles! I have thrown the world down on its face for you, do not revive it after I am gone!

They once said to [Jesus], "How is it that you can walk on water but we cannot?" He asked, "How do you value the *dīnār* and the *dirham*?" They replied "Highly!" He said. "To me they are like pebbles and dust."

He once rested his head on a stone. Satan came to him saying, "O Jesus! You have found comfort in this world!" So he cast the stone at him, saying, "This is all I had of it!"

On another occasion he was exposed to heavy rain, with lightning and thunder. He saw a tent and headed towards it, but found a woman there and so departed. Then he saw a cave and went to it, but a lion was there. He said, "O God! To each of these You have provided refuge, but to me You gave no refuge!" And God revealed to him, "Your refuge is in the resting place of My mercy. I shall give you thousands of *ḥūrīs* to marry and I shall feed the people of the Garden thousands of years for your wedding."

And Jesus said:

O Son of Adam! If what you desire from this world is what should suffice you, a little should suffice you; but if you desire more than your sufficiency, the entire world will not suffice you. Do not ruin yourselves by pursuing this world. Control your egos by abandoning what the world contains, for you have entered it naked and naked you will leave it. Ask God for provision one day at a time and know that God has made this world brief; what remains of it is a brief spell of what was already brief. Furthermore, what was limpid of it has already been drunk and only turbidity remains. And know that this world is a dwelling of punishment and illusion, so be in it as a man nursing his wound. He endures the pain of medicine, hoping for cure and freedom from illness. Let not what you see of this world lure you away from the Hereafter that you do not see!

And Jesus ﷺ said, "Strange is your working for this world, when your provision comes to you without work, and your not working for the Hereafter, when you will not be provided in it save by working."

The world showed itself to Jesus ﷺ in the form of an elaborately adorned woman. He asked her, "Do you have a husband?" She said, "Many!" He asked, "Have they all divorced you, died, and left you, or have you killed them all?" She said, "I have killed them all!" He asked her, "Did you grieve over any of them?" She replied, "They grieve over me, but I do not grieve over them. They weep over me, but I do not weep over them!" He said, "Strange how your remaining husbands do not learn from your past ones."

Jesus ﷺ once passed by a group of people who were all worshipping God, except one who was asleep. He said, "O you! Arise and worship God with your companions!" He replied, "I have worshipped him with better than their worship, I have renounced the world!" Jesus ﷺ then said, "Sleep contentedly, for you have outstripped the worshippers!"

He was asked about the saints of God, who "have no fear, neither do they grieve," so he replied:

> They are those who look at the inward of this world, while people look at its outward. They concentrate on what is to come after the world, while people concentrate on what is in it now. They destroy that which they fear might destroy them and abandon that which they know will abandon them.

Whatever contingent pleasure comes their way they refuse; whatever deceitful eminence comes to them they put down. Their world is worn out, but they do not renew it; it is in ruin among them, but they do not rebuild it; it is dead in their breasts, but they do not revive it. On the contrary, they demolish it to build their life-to-come, sell it to buy what is to remain theirs. They look at its people, afflicted with misfortunes, fallen down, and see no safety short of what they hope for, no fear other than what they fear.

This brings to completion *The Treatise of Mutual Reminding among Brothers and Attached Ones, People of Goodness and Religion*. I have only entitled it this way because it was written for mutual reminding with them. May God inspire us and them with guidance and protect us from the evil in ourselves.

Everything quoted in this treatise, whether Prophetic or other traditions, was taken from authentic authoritative books. The hadiths quoted in the conclusion are about twenty in number, but by omitting to separate them from each other they seem to be four or five. I did this believing it would be briefer and more likely to produce the desired effect.

All praise belongs to God, to whom belongs all that is in the heavens and earth. Praise is His in the Hereafter and He is the Wise, the Aware. He knows what enters the earth and what comes out of it, what comes down from the sky and what ascends in it, and He is the Compassionate, the Forgiving (QURAN, 34:1-2).

And may God's blessings and peace be upon our master Muḥammad, his Family, and Companions, until the Day of Resurrection and Arising, and may peace be upon the Messengers, and praise is for God, Lord of the Worlds.

Dictation of this treatise was completed on Sunday, before noon, the first day of Jumāda al-Awwal, a month of the year 1069 of the Prophet's emigration, may the best of blessings and peace be upon him, and praise is for God, Lord of the Worlds.

NOTES

(For the "Translator's Introduction" and Mutual Reminding*)*

1. *Taqwā* is rendered throughout this book as "the fear of God." The literal meaning of the word is *protection*. To have *taqwā* is thus to protect oneself. That this protection is from God's wrath and its consequent chastisement is implicit, not explicit. To render it as the "fear of God" is to make explicit what was implicit and leave out part of the meaning. For *taqwā* is not simply *fear*, for it may arise out of intense love and, therefore, the desire to avoid displeasing the Beloved in any manner, even if no chastisement is involved.

2. We have opted for "spiritual disciple" for the Arabic word *murīd*. Other options were *seeker*, *aspirant*, and *traveler* or *wayfarer*. None is fully satisfactory. A *murīd* is he who desires or demands something. *Murīdu'llāh* is one who yearns for God, while *murīdu'l-ākhira* is one who desires Paradise in the Hereafter. Acting upon these wishes means traveling the Path. A serious seeker of God must become a disciple and receive instruction and training under an authorized master.

3. *By the afternoon! Man is indeed in loss, except those who believe, do good, counsel each other to truth and counsel each other to patience* (QURAN, 103:1-3).

4. *Help one another in benevolence and godfearingness and help not one another in sin and transgression, and fear God...* (QURAN, 5:2).

5. *Indeed, the most honorable among you in the sight of God are those who fear Him most* (QURAN, 49:13).

6. *But God is the Protector of the God-fearing* (QURAN, 45:19).

7. *I have created jinn and mankind only that they may worship Me* (QURAN, 51:56).

8. *So extol the praises of your Lord and be among those who prostrate, and worship your Lord until what is certain comes to you* (QURAN, 15:98-99).

9. One of the necessary conditions of the Friday sermon or *khuṭba* is to counsel the audience, and it is sufficient counsel to exhort them to fear God.

10. *Taqwā*, when sincere, leads to excellence in obedience. Excellence was defined by the Prophet ﷺ as "to worship God as if you see Him, for if you see Him not, He sees you." God wishes to see His servants engaged in doing what pleases Him and avoiding what displeases Him. God is entirely aware of His servants' states, both inwardly and outwardly, but His gaze falls upon them according to these states: it can be a gaze of mercy and solicitude, or one of displeasure leading to punishment.

11. The literal meaning of *walī* is *ally* or both *protector* and *protégé*. The term has a general meaning based upon the verse, *God is the Protector of the believers; He brings them out from the darknesses into the light* (QURAN, 2:257). In this sense, every believer is a *walī* of God. However, those who make God their sole ally and strive sincerely to please Him become His protégés in a much more intense and specific way that is indicated in the hadith, "My servant ceases not to draw nearer to Me with supererogatory devotions until I love him, when I love him I become his eyesight with which he sees, his hearing with which he hears, his hand with which he strikes, and his foot on which he walks. When he asks of Me, I grant him; and when he seeks My protection, I protect him." Thus when one speaks of a *walī*, one usually means a beloved one of God, a person who has become the object of special Divine solicitude and grace.

12. It is in a believer's nature to love that which God loves and to detest that which God detests. Thus, a believer will detest ugliness and chaos, which in the context of human behavior is willful disobedience to God, leading to all kinds of evil and sin. But a believer detests only evil thoughts, feelings, and deeds, never a human being as such, or for that matter any other created being. Human beings belong to their Creator; they are attributed to Him. He treats them with mercy, providing for them generously, even as they disobey and rebel against Him. The believer must of necessity model his feelings and behavior on his Lord's. He may thus disapprove of someone's behavior, but this should never prevent him from treating him with gentleness and courtesy, helping him when in need, counseling him whenever appropriate, and imploring God to guide him to the straight path.

Mutual Reminding

13. The meaning of Imām ʿAlī's words seems to be that one should perform what one is currently doing to perfection, allowing ample time for it, rather than being in a hurry to get it over with and move on to the next task.
14. Illicit or suspect food includes food bought with illicit or suspect money.
15. Things of this world are called "debris" because they are invariably imperfect, have noxious side effects, and are evanescent— shortly to be discarded, either because of boredom or decay.
16. The ruin in question here is the ruin of the love of the world in the heart of Muslims, the ruin of that attachment, for that leads to working for it at the expense of working for one's life-to-come. It means that whatever is done for the world has to be done with detachment and appropriate frugality. It does not mean letting one's worldly affairs go to ruin, nor attending to them with less than utmost efficacy. Were it not so, there would have been no Islamic civilization, for this civilization was created by men who feared God and were quite incapable of acting in a manner that ran contrary to the instructions of the Quran and the Prophet ﷺ.
17. These metaphors refer to death.
18. This is a hadith found in al-Tirmidhī.
19. *Riyāʾ*, rendered here as *ostentation*, is to act to be seen by others.
20. Idolatry is *shirk*, that is, to associate other than God with Him in worship. This is the "greater idolatry." The '"lesser idolatry" is to worship Him with something other than Him as part of your intention.
21. What is meant here is one's worldly situation as a whole, including one's social position, family, and possessions.
22. Thaʿlaba was a hypocrite who lived in the time of the Prophet ﷺ. In those days, a hypocrite was one who professed to be a Muslim, yet harbored disbelief in his heart. Thaʿlaba once asked the Prophet ﷺ for a large number of sheep, promising to pay his obligatory *Zakāt* and give of them in charitable ways. His flock prospered and increased so much that he had to take them away from town to a valley that could suffice them. When the time came for him to pay his *Zakāt*, he refused, repeating his refusal more than once, thus becom-

ing accursed for having broken his promise to God and His Prophet ﷺ, barring himself from the way to repent or return to Islam.

23. *Surely in that there is a reminder to him who has a heart or will listen with attentiveness* (QURAN, 50:37).

24. Hārūt and Mārūt are the two fallen angels who tempted the people of Babylon by teaching them how to make magic. But they always warned them first that to make magic was tantamount to disbelief. However, the attraction of what they taught was so great that people still went to them to learn, even having understood that to do so meant permanent punishment in Hell. *And that which was sent down to Hārūt and Mārūt, the two angels at Babylon. Nor did they teach it to anyone until they had said, "We are only a temptation, so do not disbelieve!"* (QURAN, 2:102).

25. That is, he who is forgetful of God and the Hereafter but is never forgotten by God who watches his every movement.

26. *Al-Firdaws*, rendered here as *Paradise*, is the highest degree of the Garden.

GOOD MANNERS

*The Treatise on the Good Manners
of the Spiritual Disciple's Wayfaring*

PROLOGUE

In the name of God, the All-Merciful, the Compassionate

All ability and strength are only by God, the High, the Formidable. Praise belongs to God, who, when He wills, casts into the hearts of seekers the anguish of longing, thereby driving them to travel the path to happiness, which is faith, worship, and the extinction of all formalism and habits.

May God send His blessings and peace upon our master Muḥammad, the master of masters, and upon his family and Companions, who themselves are masters and leaders.

God the Exalted has said (who is more truthful than He!), *Whoever desires the immediate, We shall hasten what We will of it to whomever We will; then We shall appoint for him Hell, in which he will be plunged, blamed, and defeated. And whoever desires the Hereafter and earnestly strives for it, and he is a believer—these shall have their strivings rewarded* (QURAN, 17:18-19). The *immediate* as mentioned here is this fleeting world. Therefore, the one who [merely] desires this world, let alone actively pursues it, ends up in the Fire, blamed and belittled. Should not a man of reason beware and turn away from it?

The *Hereafter* here means the Garden [or Heaven]. It is not enough to merely desire it in order to gain it. Faith and good works are both necessary, as is indicated in the passage, *and earnestly strives for it, and he is a believer*. The *strivings* to be rewarded are those deeds that are accepted by God, thereby deserving praise and such great rewards without limits nor endings—all by the grace of God and His mercy.

The complete loser is the seeker of this world, whose end was described in the Quran. His desire for the world is so powerful that it causes him to forget and deny the Hereafter. He is a disbeliever, and he will be in Hell forever. The one who acknowledges the Hereafter but does not strive for it is astray and yet another loser. The Messenger of God ﷺ has said, "Deeds depend on intentions; each man receives according to what he has intended. He whose migration was for the sake of God and His Messenger, then he has migrated for God and His Messenger. He whose migration is for worldly things that he wishes to acquire or for a woman he wishes to marry, then he has migrated for that which he had intended."

The Prophet ﷺ thus informed us that [one's] deed is only as valid as the intention behind it, and that people are rewarded according to their intentions. When these [intentions] are good, they receive nothing but good. When these are evil, they receive nothing but evil. He whose intention is good, his deed then is inevitably good, and he whose intention is malicious, his deed is inevitably malicious, even if it appears good outwardly, as in the case of a man who behaves in a righteous way only to appear righteous in the eyes of people.

The Prophet ﷺ also informed us that he who acts for the sake of God by following in the footsteps of the Messenger of God ﷺ, his reward is with God, who will be pleased with him and make his last abode His Garden—near Him and in the company of the best of His people. Those whose intentions are directed toward other than God and who act as such, their rewards are with those to whom their intentions are directed, those they performed for, those who can neither benefit nor harm them or anybody else, those who can cause neither life, death, nor the resurrection. The Prophet ﷺ elected to speak of "migration" by way of providing an example. As it is well known to people of understanding, rules such as these can be generalized to all the laws of Islam.

I now say this: Know, O disciple, O seeker, who is intent on directing himself [toward God], that when you requested me to send you some of our teachings, I found nothing [ready] that could suit your purpose. Therefore, I decided to record brief chapters containing some of the good manners of discipleship, in an accessible manner of expression.

It is God whom I ask to benefit me, you, and all other brothers with what He will inspire in me of this matter and allow me to reach. He is my sufficiency and the best of Guardians.

ONE

The Beginning of the Path is a Powerful Urge of Divine Origin Which Should be Strengthened, Protected, and Responded To

Know that the path begins when a powerful urge is cast into the heart of the servant which troubles and unnerves him, and drives him towards God and the last abode. It turns him away from this world and from being, like others, engaged in amassing and grooming it, tasting and enjoying its pleasures, and being deceived by its ornaments. This urge is one of the hidden warriors of God; it is a gift of solicitude and a sign of right guidance. It is often bestowed upon a servant as he listens to those people who stir in him the fear [of God] as well as desire and yearning [for Him], and when he looks at the men of God and they look at him. It can be given without cause.

It is commanded and encouraged to actively subject oneself to receive such gifts, for to expect to receive something when not standing at the door and subjecting oneself therein is foolish and unintelligent. The Messenger of God ﷺ said, "Your Lord has gifts in these days of your time, subject yourself to receive them!"

He whom God honors with such a noble urge must know how precious it is. Let him also know that it is one of the greatest favors of God, Exalted is He, such that he will never fully know how truly precious it is, nor will he ever be able to show gratitude enough for it. So let him thank God, Exalted is He, to his utmost for having selected him from among his peers to receive it. How many a Muslim reaches the age of eighty or more and neither finds this yearning nor is affected by it a single day of his life!

A disciple [*murīd*] should do his best to strengthen, protect, and respond to this urge. Strengthening it is by remembering God often, reflecting on what He has, and keeping the company of the people of God. Protecting it is by keeping away from the company of those who are veiled and by ignoring the insinuations of devils. Responding to it is by hastening to return to God and sincerely seeking His nearness—by neither waiting, postponing, procrastinating, nor delaying. This is a chance that one is given and should seize; the door is now open for him, and he should enter. He is being called, and he should be swift. Let him beware of letting one day pass after the other, for this is the work of the Devil. He must advance and not weaken. He must refuse manufacturing excuses, such as saying that there is no time or that he is not good enough for the task. Abū'l-Rabīʿ, may God have mercy on him, said, "Go to God with your limps and your broken limbs. Do not wait for full health for that would only be idleness."

Imām Ibn ʿAṭā'illāh said in his *Ḥikam*, "To say that the work must be postponed until one is free is but the idleness of the soul."

TWO

Repentance, its Conditions, and Protecting Oneself from Sins

A disciple on the path to God should begin with sound repentance from all his sins. If he has treated unjustly any of God's creation, he should correct this by giving everyone their due. If this is not possible, he should ask them to release him from those obligations. Whoever is encumbered with debts to creation cannot proceed towards the Real.

It is a condition for sound repentance that one feel sincere remorse for his sins and be wholly determined not to repeat such actions as long as he lives. If he does not refrain from them, or is still harboring the intention to repeat them, his repentance is false.

A disciple should always be extremely aware of his shortcomings towards his Lord. When these shortcomings bring him sadness and his heart breaks, let him know that God is with him, for He says, Transcendent is He, "I am with those whose hearts break for My sake."

A disciple should protect himself from the smallest of sins—let alone the major ones—with more urgency than protecting himself from lethal poison. Should he commit [such a sin], he should be more frightened than if he had taken poison, for sins are to the heart what poison is to the body. The heart of a disciple is more precious to him than his body. A disciple has no capital other than protecting and improving his heart. The body is a target for disease, soon to be destroyed by death. Its death, however, means only that one has to leave this grief and anxiety-laden world. But if the heart is ruined, the Hereafter is ruined. The only one to be rescued from the wrath of God and gain His rewards and win His pleasure will be the one who comes to Him with a heart that is "whole."

THREE

Guarding the Heart Against Insinuations, Ailments, and Ill-Thinking

A disciple should strive to guard his heart against insinuations, ailments, and bad thoughts. He should guard its gate by constant vigilance and prevent these things from entering. Once they enter his heart, they will ruin it and it becomes difficult to expel them. He should purify his heart—which is the place his Lord's gaze falls upon—from worldly desires, spite, rancor, deceitfulness, or thinking ill of any Muslim. He must be of good advice to them, compassionate, and merciful; he must think well of them all, desiring for them whatever good he desires for himself, and disliking for them whatever evil he dislikes for himself.

Know, disciple, that the heart commits sins which are uglier, fouler, and more offensive than those committed by the senses: a heart remains unfit for the gnosis of God and for His love to descend into it, until it rids itself of all such things.

Among the worst sins of the heart are arrogance, ostentation, and resentful envy. Arrogance is proof of great foolishness, excessive ignorance, and stupidity. Arrogance does not become one who knows that he was made from a drop of fetid semen and soon enough will end up a decaying corpse. If he possesses virtues and good qualities, they are but gracious gifts from God; a person can achieve nothing by his own power, neither can he acquire anything through his own strength and cleverness. When he behaves with arrogance toward the servants of God, employing therein the gifts that God has graciously bestowed on him, does he not fear that by behaving discourteously and attributing to himself what belongs to God, He would take away everything from him? Prominence and greatness are attributes of God, the Compeller, the Supreme.

The presence of ostentation is proof that the heart is devoid of the vastness and majesty of God because it seeks the approval of creatures through feigning and is not content with the knowledge that God, the Lord of creation, knows all that he does. The one who performs good deeds and likes it to be known, so that people would revere and serve him, is an ignorant hypocrite whose desire is but for this world. The detached man is one who finds it repugnant when people offer him reverence and wealth, and seeks to avoid them. Who can be more ignorant than one who seeks the

Hereafter by acts of this world? If he is unable to renounce the world, he should seek it from its Owner. The hearts of creation are in the hand of God; He makes them incline toward the one who seeks Him, and He makes them serve him.

As for resentful envy, it is manifest enmity to God, and opposition to Him in His Kingdom. When [God] the Exalted bestows gifts on some of His servants, it is evidence that He intends them to be given them and has chosen them for them, for none forces His hand. If the servant wants something different from what his Lord wants, he is discourteous and deserves to come to grief.

Resentful envy can also target things associated with the Hereafter, such as knowledge and virtue. It is ugly of a disciple to be jealous or to resent a companion on the path who has given him help. On the contrary, he should rejoice for the help he receives from his companion, and derive strength from the fact that they are alike. A believer finds strength in his brother. What a disciple should do is inwardly desire and outwardly act to gather people on the path to God and [help in their] submitting to Him. He should not care whether they become better than him or he better than them, for this is given by God, and He, Exalted is He, selects whom He will for His mercy.

The blameworthy qualities of the heart, are many. We have not mentioned them all for the sake of brevity, but we have cautioned against the major sources producing them. The origin, foundation, and root of them all is love of this world. Its love is the head of every sin, as has been handed down. When the heart is free from it, it becomes healthy and clear, enlightened and fragrant, fit to receive the lights and have the secrets unveiled.

FOUR

Guarding the Senses Against Transgressions and Against Being Deceived by This World

A disciple should strive to restrain his senses and limbs from transgressions and sins, and only use them in obedience. He should use them only in those things which would benefit him in the Hereafter. He should take great care in guarding his tongue, for its size is small, but its crimes are great. Let him prevent it from lying, backbiting, and other forms of forbidden speech. Let him beware of lewdness, and of delving into what does not concern him, even if it were not forbidden, for it hardens the heart and wastes time. A disciple should not only move his tongue in reciting the Quran, the remembrance of God, giving advice to a Muslim, enjoining good, and forbidding evil, but also only for those worldly things that relate to the Hereafter. The Prophet ﷺ said, "The speech of the Son of Adam will be counted against him, not for him, except for enjoining good, forbidding evil, and remembering God."

Know that hearing and eyesight are two open doors, whatever enters through them reaches the heart. How many a thing does a man hear or see, which he should not have, but that once they have entered the heart, it proves difficult to remove them? For the heart is rapidly affected by what enters it, then the effect is difficult to erase. Let the disciple then be careful to protect his hearing and eyesight, and strive to restrain all his senses and his limbs from sins and from what is in excess of the necessary. Let him beware of looking with approval at the ornaments of this world, for its outward is deception and its inward is a lesson in wisdom. The eye looks at its deceptive manifestations, but the heart looks at the lesson hidden within. How many a disciple looked at some of the beauties of this world and his heart leaned toward them, liked them, and became inclined to build and acquire. So lower your eyes, disciple, and look at creation only with the intention of seeing the lesson within it. Remember as you look that it will wither and go from whence it came. It came from nonexistence. It was gazed upon by many people who are now gone, while it still remains. Generation after generation have received it as an inheritance. Look at creatures with an eye that sees them as evidence of their Creator's perfect power. Every creation says with the tongue of its state, "There is no god but God, the August, the Wise." This is what the people of enlightened hearts—who perceive by the light of God—can hear.

FIVE

Remaining in a State of Purity and Preferring Hunger to Satiety

A disciple should maintain a state of purity, and whenever he loses it should perform his ritual ablutions followed by two *rakʿa*s. When he is intimate with his wife, he must take immediate *ghusl* and not remain impure. He should make it easy for himself to maintain ritual purity by eating little, for the one who eats much breaks his *wuḍū'* often and finds it an effort to maintain purity. Eating little is also of help in keeping awake at night, which is one of the most important activities of a disciple. He should eat only when necessary and sleep only when it overcomes him. He should speak only when necessary and mix only with people from whom he can benefit. The one who eats much, his heart grows hard, and his limbs become too heavy for acts of worship. Eating much makes one sleep and talk much. When a disciple sleeps much and talks much, his quest becomes an empty shell devoid of substance.

A hadith states, "The Son of Adam never fills a vessel worse than his stomach. It should suffice the Son of Adam a few morsels to keep his back straight. If he must, then a third [of his stomach] for his food, a third for his beverage, and a third for his breath."

SIX

Directing One's Whole Attention to God and Devoting Oneself to His Worship

A disciple should be the furthest of people from sins and forbidden acts, the most conscientious in carrying out his obligations, the most eager to do what draws him nearer to God, and the swiftest in performing acts of goodness.

A disciple differs from other people only in attending wholly to God, being obedient, and freeing himself from everything that may distract him from His devotions. Let him spend his breaths carefully, hold on to his time avariciously, and only expend it in what takes him nearer to God and benefits him on the Day he meets Him. He should have a daily *wird*[1] of every kind of worship, so that he will have a number of those to hold on to tenaciously and never allow any of them to be neglected, however difficult his circumstances. He should recite the Magnificent Quran frequently, reflect on its meanings and chant its words correctly. While reciting he should be full of the immensity of the Speaker, unlike those who recite with expert tongues and loud voices but are distracted and have hearts which harbor neither exaltation nor reverence for God. They read it in the form it was sent down, from its opening to its end, yet know nothing of its meanings, nor of the reasons why each verse was revealed. Had they known, they would have acted: knowledge alone is of no use. One who is ignorant and one who knows but does not act on his knowledge are no different, except that the latter will have a stronger case made against him before God. Seen in this light, the ignorant is in a better situation. This is why it was said, "Ignorance is better than knowledge that is of no benefit."

O disciple, have a share in Night Prayers, for the night is the time when the servant is alone with his Lord. Make abundant pleas for help and forgiveness. Commune with your Lord with the tongue of the humble and needy, and a heart where complete helplessness and abasement are realized. Beware of neglecting night worship, for dawn must always find you awake and remembering God, Transcendent and Exalted is He!

SEVEN

Excellence in the Performance of Ritual Prayers, Presence with God is the Essence of all Acts of Worship

O disciple, strive to your utmost to make your performance of the five Prayers satisfactory, and do that by making your standing, recitation, humility, bowing, prostrations, and the Prayers' other obligations and *sunna*s complete in every way.

Before entering into Prayer, bring to your heart the awesomeness of the One you wish to stand before, Majestic and High is He. Beware of communing with the King of kings, the Subduer of tyrants, with a distracted heart, deeply lost in the valleys of unawareness and whisperings, roaming the places of incidental thoughts and worldly ideas; you would thus deserve to be hateful to God and expelled from His doorstep.

The Messenger ﷺ has said, "When a servant stands up to pray, God turns His face toward him. Should the servant look behind him, God the Exalted, says, 'The Son of Adam has turned towards a better than I!' Should the servant turn away again, God says the same. When he looks away for the third time, God turns away from him and abandons him." If this is the state of one who looks away physically, what about one who when in Prayer directs his heart to the fortunes and beauties of this world? God, Transcendent and Exalted is He, looks at hearts and secrets, not at forms and appearances.

Know that the essence and meaning of worship is presence

with God. Acts of worship which are devoid of presence are like dust, easily blown away. The one who is not present with God in worship is like the one who offers as gift to a great king an empty coffer or a dead maid! How deserving will such a man be of punishment and being deprived of reward!

EIGHT

Cautioning Against Neglecting the Friday Prayer and Other Congregational Prayers, and Exhorting to Keep the Regular Supererogatory Prayers

Beware greatly, O disciple, of leaving the Friday and other congregational Prayers, for such is the pattern of the indolent and the mark of the ignorant. Take care to perform the regular supererogatory Prayers before and after the obligatory ones; persevere with the *Witr* and *Ḍuḥā* Prayers and with keeping alive the interval between the two night Prayers, through remembrance [of God].

Be extremely careful to always keep alive the periods between the dawn prayer and sunrise, and between the afternoon prayer and sunset, for these are noble times where those servants who turn to God receive the flow of His assistance. The time following the dawn prayer, when kept alive, has a powerful and specific effect in attracting material provision, whereas, the time following the afternoon prayer, if kept alive, has a powerful effect in attracting provisions for the heart. This has been experienced by the people of clear vision among the great gnostics.

A hadith states, "The one who sits where he has just prayed, remembering God after the Dawn Prayer, is quicker to receive his provision than the one who travels the horizons [seeking provision]."

NINE
Exhorting to Perseverance in Remembrance and Reflection

What really counts on the path of God the Exalted, having obeyed commands and avoided forbidden things, is to persevere in remembering God; so keep to it, O disciple, in all situations, with heart and tongue, at all times and places.

The invocation which contains the meaning of all invocations and their fruits, invisible and visible, is *Lā ilāha illa'llāh*. This is the invocation which people of beginnings are enjoined to keep and which people of ending return to.

He who would delight in tasting some of the secrets of the path and having some of its realities unveiled before him, let him be intent on remembering God, the Exalted, with a heart that is present, courtesy that is abundant, attention that is sincere, and concentration that is piercing. Whenever these are combined in a person, to him is revealed the highest *Malakūt*, his spirit beholds the realities of the World of Utmost Purity, and the eye of his secret witnesses the Highest and Holiest Beauty.

And reflect in abundance, O disciple. Reflection is of three kinds. The first is reflection on the wonders of [Divine] Power and the marvels of the heavenly and earthly kingdoms. And its fruit is gnosis of God. The second is reflection on the gifts of God and His graces. And its fruit is the love of God. The third is reflection on this world, the next, and the states of creation in both. And its benefit is turning away from this world and becoming attentive to the Hereafter. We have discoursed on the various avenues of reflection in the *Book of Assistance* where they can be found by those who want them.

TEN
How to Rebuke the Soul From Being Lazy in Obedience and Inclined Towards Disobedience

If you feel, O disciple, that your soul, through laziness and sloth, moves away from submission and good actions, then lead it back by the reins of hope, remind it of what God has promised those who obey Him: vast bounty, permanent bliss, grace, and contentment, eternity in the vastness of the Garden, honor, and high rank and eminence accorded by God the Exalted and His servants.

If you feel that your soul is leaning toward rebellion or heading for sin, then use the whip of fear to rebuke it. Remind it of that with which God has threatened those who disobey Him: humiliation, calamity, debasement and vengeance, expulsion and deprivation, dejection and loss.

Beware of falling into the error of those who strayed and belittled the Garden and the Fire! Magnify what God and His Messenger have magnified and act only for the sake of God, for He is your Lord and you are His slave. Ask Him to let you enter His Garden and ask His protection from His Fire by His grace and mercy.

Should the Devil—may God curse him!—tell you that God, Transcendent and High is He, neither needs you nor your deeds, that neither your submission will benefit Him, nor your rebellion harm Him, reply to him, "This is true! But I am the one in need of the graces of God and the good deeds. I am the one who benefits by submission and is harmed from disobedience. This is what my Lord has said to me in His Noble Book and on the tongue of His Messenger ﷺ." If [the Devil] then says to you, "If, in the knowledge of God, you are among the fortunate, you will inevitably end up in the Garden, whether you submit or rebel; and if, in the knowledge of God, you are among the wretched, you will end up in the Fire, even if you are obedient!" You must ignore him for the decree is hidden, only God knows and none of creation has anything to do with it. Submission and obedience are the surest proof of good fortune, nothing stands between the obedient and the Garden should he die in a state of obedience. Whereas disobedience is the surest proof of wretchedness, nothing stands between the sinner and the Fire should he die in a state of sin.

ELEVEN
The States of the Soul and Being Patient

Know, disciple, that the beginning of the path is patience, and its end is thankfulness. Its beginning is difficulty, and its end is bliss. Its beginning is toil and weariness, and its end is opening, unveiling, and arrival at the ultimate goal which is gnosis of God, arrival to Him, being comforted by Him, and standing in His noble Presence with His angels standing before Him. The one who makes gracious patience the foundation of all his affairs attains to every goodness, reaches everything that he hopes for, and wins all that he seeks.

Know that to begin with, the soul is "inciting," it exhorts to evil and forbids good. When one resists its commands and patiently endures what comes from contradicting its whims, it becomes a "reproachful" soul. The reproachful soul is changeful because it has two faces, one "serene" and the other "inciting." It can be this on one occasion, and that on another. If one then gently guides it and leads it by the reins of desire for what God has in store, it becomes serene, enjoining good and finding its pleasure and comfort in it, and forbidding evil and being repelled and fleeing from it.

The one whose soul is serene is greatly amazed by the way people turn away from acts of obedience and [turn away] what they bring on of delight, comfort, and pleasure; and then they rush into rebellion and lusts and what they hold of grief, estrangement, and bitterness. [The possessor of the serene soul] may think that the way they taste these two states is the same as his; he then draws on his own experience for comparison and remembers how pleasurable he had once found it to satisfy his lusts, and how bitter to perform acts of obedience; then he understands that he had only reached his present state after a long struggle, and by the immense grace of God.

You now know that it is but *patience* to stay away from sins and lustful desires and to keep to acts of obedience that makes you reach everything that is good, every noble station, and every lofty state. Has [God] not said, Transcendent and High is He, *O you who believe, have patience, persevere, be vigilant, and fear God, that you may succeed!* (QURAN, 3:200)? And He said, Exalted is He, *And the gracious word of your Lord was fulfilled in the Children of Israel because of their patience* (QURAN, 7:137); and He said, *And We made of them leaders to guide by Our command, when they had patience and certainty in Our signs* (QURAN, 32:24). And a hadith says, "Certainty and determined patience are among what you possess the least. The one who has a share of these is not worried by what he misses in night worship and day fasting."

TWELVE

Heeding the Example of the People of Fortitude— Provision is Apportioned

A disciple may be put through the hardships of poverty, need, and the narrowing of the channels of provision. He should thank God and consider this a great blessing. For this world is an enemy, and God pushes it towards His enemies, but deflects it away from His protégés. Let him thank God for making him resemble His prophets, saints, and virtuous servants.

The Master of Messengers and the best of creation,

Good Manners

Muḥammad, may the blessings of God and His peace be upon him, used to tie a stone to his stomach out of hunger. Two months and more would pass and no fire would be lit in his house—neither for cooking, nor for any other purpose. He survived on dates and water. One day he received a guest, so he sent for food to each of his nine houses, but none was found. When he died he left his armor pawned with a Jew for a few measures of barley which was on that day all that there was to eat in his house.

O disciple, let your worldly requirements be no more than a cloth to cover what should be covered and a morsel of licit food to allay your hunger. Beware of the deadly poison of longing for worldly luxuries and pleasures and of envying those who enjoy them, for they will be asked to account for what they took and enjoyed. If you knew the hardships they have to endure, the bitterness they have to swallow, the troubles and anxieties they have to carry in their hearts and breasts, all of which come from pursuing the world, nurturing it, and guarding it carefully, you would see clearly that these far outweigh the pleasures enjoyed, if indeed pleasures there are.

It is enough to repel you from loving the world to know that God, Exalted is He, says, *Were it not that people would have become all alike, We would have given those who disbelieve in the All-Merciful silver roofs for their houses and stairways to climb on, and for their houses doors [of silver] and couches on which to recline, and ornaments of gold. These are but the fleeting pleasures of the world, while the Hereafter is with your Lord for the God-fearing* (QURAN, 43:33-35). And the Messenger of God ﷺ said, "This world is the prison of the believer and the Garden of the disbeliever. Had it been worth the wing of a gnat to God, He would never have allowed a disbeliever a sip of its water." And [it is enough] to know that since He created it, He has never looked at it.

Know that provision is divided and allocated by [Divine] decree. Some servants are given a large share, some small. This is the wisdom of God. If, O disciple, you are one whose share is small, have patience and be content. Be pleased with what God has allotted to you. If you are one of those who have received a large share, take what you need and spend the rest in ways of goodness and benevolence.

THIRTEEN

Moving Toward God is Compatible With Earning, Divesting Oneself of the Means of Livelihood is Not Required

Know that it is not necessary for a man who wishes to enter the path to God to leave his wealth, craft, or commerce. What is necessary for him is to fear God in what he does, and to have moderation in pursuing his livelihood so as not to miss obligatory or supererogatory acts of worship. Neither should he fall into the forbidden, nor the superfluous which is of no help on the way to God.

Should the disciple know that his heart would not be firm, nor his religion safe, except by shedding off his wealth and all other means, then this becomes incumbent upon him. If he has wives and children who require expenditure and clothes, he has to provide their needs and strive for this. If he becomes incapable of doing so due to any of the reasons acceptable by *Sharīʿa*, he will be blameless and safe from sin.

O disciple, know that only when you realize that your days in this world are few and your death near, will you be capable of acts of obedience, of avoiding lusts, and of turning away from this world. Keep your ultimate end before your eyes, make ready for death, and know that it may descend upon you at any moment. Beware of long hopes, for they sway you toward the love of this world and make it difficult for you to persevere in obedience. Be intent on worship or devote yourself to the path of the Hereafter.

From the realization of the nearness of death and the brevity of time comes all good. Seek this, may God grant you and us success!

FOURTEEN

Being Patient When Harmed by Others and Being Wary of Being Tempted by Them

People sometimes show hostility to a disciple. They may hurt him, treat him harshly, or talk about him disparagingly. Should you become afflicted by any such thing, you must remain patient, forsake retaliation, and maintain your heart pure of grudges and evil intentions. Beware of asking God to send down His wrath on those who injure you. Should they happen to suffer a mishap, never say, "It is because of what they did to me."

Even better than to endure injury with equanimity is to forgive and ask God to increase them, for such is the behavior of the *ṣiddiqūn*.

When creation shuns you, consider this to be a blessing from your Lord, for if people come to you, they may distract you from His obedience. Should you become afflicted by their coming to you, respecting and praising you, beware of the effect this may have on you, and thank God for hiding your faults from them. If you feel that they are distracting you from God, or if you fear the imprint of affectation upon yourself and strive to appear fairer in their eyes, then shut your door and isolate yourself, or else leave the place where you are known for [a place] where you are unknown.

Always opt for anonymity. Flee fame and publicity. They are a test and a hardship. One of our predecessors said, "By God! A servant, if truthful with God, will always love to pass unnoticed." Another has said, "I have never known a man to wish to become known but that his religion quit him and he became exposed."

FIFTEEN
Getting Rid of the Need to Obtain People's Approval

O disciple, strive to purify your heart both from the fear of people and from putting your hopes in them, for this would make you remain silent when faced with falsehood, compromise your religion, and neglect enjoining good and forbidding evil. This would be ample humiliation. A believer is strong by his Lord; he feels no fear nor hope except with regard to Him.

When one of your brother Muslims offers you something by way of showing affection, take it if you need it, but thank God, for He is the real giver, and thank the one whom God has chosen to deliver it to you. If you do not need it, see whether it would be better for your heart to take it or refuse it. If you refuse, do it tactfully so as not to hurt the heart of the giver, for the feelings of a Muslim are of consequence to God.

Beware of refusing for the sake of acquiring a reputation, or of accepting for your appetites. However, to accept for your appetites is better than turning something down to acquire a reputation of asceticism and of turning away from the world. The truthful will not be confused, for his Lord gives him a light in his heart by which he knows what is required of him.

SIXTEEN
Rebuking the Seekers of Unveilings and Supernatural Events

One of the most harmful things for a disciple is his wish for unveilings and longing for *karāmāt* and for supernatural happenings. These will never come to him as long as he desires their appearance, for they come mostly to those who have a dislike for such things and no wish for them.

Good Manners

Things can happen to certain conceited people to lure them even more and test those among them who are weak believers. In this context, these things are to debase rather than to honor. They would be considered *karāmāt* only if they appear in people of rectitude. O disciple, should God honor you with such things, then thank Him for them, Transcendent is He, do not dwell on them and become overconfident. Keep them hidden and do not mention them to other people. If none appears to you, do not wish for them, nor grieve for their absence.

Know that the *karāma* that encompasses every other *karāma*, whether of realities or forms, is rectitude, which manifests in complying with [God's] commands and avoiding what is forbidden, outwardly and inwardly. Strive to fully achieve those qualities, and then the higher and lower worlds will serve you, but in such a way as not to veil you from your Lord, nor distract you from what He wants for you.

SEVENTEEN
Seeking Provision and Striving For It

O disciple, think well of your Lord. Think that He will help you fulfill your needs, guard and protect you, and entrust you neither to creation nor to yourself. He has informed us that He is as good to His servant as His servant thinks Him to be.

Remove from your heart the fear of poverty and the expectation that one day you may need people. Beware of directing your whole attention to such matters. Trust in your Lord's promise and His providing for you. He says, Exalted is He, *Nothing walks the earth but that God provides for it* (QURAN, 11:6). And you are one of those who walk the earth, so occupy yourself with what He has commanded you rather than with what He has already guaranteed for you, for your Lord never forgets you. He has informed you that provision is with Him and commanded you to seek it from Him by acts of worship. He has said, Exalted is He, *Seek provision from God, and worship Him, and be thankful to Him. To Him shall you return* (QURAN, 29:17). Do you not see how He provides for those who reject Him and worship other than Him? Will He not provide for the believers who worship Him alone? When He provides for those who sin and disobey, will He not provide for the obedient ones who remember and thank Him in abundance?

EIGHTEEN

Keeping the Company of the Best of People, the Good Manners of the Disciple with His Shaykh, and the Attributes of the Perfect Shaykh

O disciple, you must take the greatest care to keep the company of the best people and to sit with the virtuous and the righteous. Search with utmost care for a good shaykh, a man of guidance and good advice, who has knowledge of *Sharīʿa*, has traveled the path of *tarīqa*, and tasted *ḥaqīqa*.[2] A man who has perfection of mind, vastness of breast, wisdom in management, knowledge of the ranks of people, and the ability to discern the variations in their instincts, innate qualities, and states. When you find him, surrender to him, give him command over all your affairs, and take his advice and suggestions in everything that concerns you. [SEE "TRANSLATOR'S APPENDIX TWO."] Follow his example in everything he says or does, except in those things which are specific to his status as a shaykh, for a shaykh has to mix with people, speak to them gently and evenly, and draw the near and far among them to God. Object not, neither publicly nor secretly, to any behavior of his. Should a disturbing thought about him enter your heart strive to cast it out. If you do not succeed, speak to the shaykh about it so that he can teach you how to rid yourself of it. You should also inform him of everything that occurs to you, especially concerning the path. Beware of obeying him publicly and when in his presence, then disobeying him in secret—you can otherwise perish.

Do not meet any shaykh known to take people on the path unless you have your shaykh's permission. If he permits you, guard your heart and meet whoever you will. If he does not, know that he has chosen what is best for you. Do not accuse him of being envious or jealous. God forbid that such may occur from [God's] people, His elect.

Beware of asking the shaykh for *karāmāt* or that he reveal to you what you secretly think. Knowledge of the hidden belongs exclusively to God. The limit of a saint is that God reveals to him some of the hidden, some of the time. A disciple may enter the presence of his shaykh wishing to be told his own thoughts and the shaykh may refrain from telling him although they are unveiled to him. This is to guard his secret and hide his state, for they are, may God be pleased with them, the most careful to guard secrets and the farthest from showing off by *karāmāt* and supernatural events, even when given command over them. Most *karāmāt* appearing on saints do not happen by choice. When any such event occurs, those who witness it are asked not to divulge what they have witnessed until the shaykh leaves the world. Saints may sometimes openly bring about such events when there is greater benefit in doing so than in keeping them hidden.

Know that a perfect shaykh is one who benefits the disciple through his spiritual power,[3] his actions, and his words. He protects him whether present or absent. If the disciple is physically far from his shaykh, he must seek from him guidelines as to what he should do and what he should refrain from doing. The most harmful thing to the disciple is a change in his shaykh's feelings toward him. If this happens, then even were the shaykhs of the East and the West to unite to improve him they would never succeed, until his own shaykh becomes pleased with him again.

Know that a disciple in search of a shaykh should not surrender command over himself to anyone said to be a shaykh and a guide on the path until he comes to know that the shaykh is worthy of this description and until he can accept him wholeheartedly. Similarly, if a disciple goes to a shaykh asking to be taken on the path, he should not be permitted to enter it until his sincerity has been tested, as well as the extent to which he thirsts for someone to guide him to his Lord.

All this relates to the shaykh of *taḥkīm*.[4] They made it a condition that the disciple remain with him like the body of a dead man in the hands of the one washing it for burial, or like a child with his mother. This does not apply to the shaykh of *tabarruk*.[5] If the disciple's intention is to gather *baraka* and not hand over command over his affairs, then the more shaykhs he meets the better.

A disciple who is not succeeding in finding a shaykh should persevere in resolutely striving. He should turn to God with total sincerity and poverty and ask Him to give him a guide. He will be answered by the One who answers those in desperate need; He will send him a servant of His to take him by the hand.

A disciple may be searching for a shaykh thinking that he is without one, while in actual fact a shaykh he has never seen is rearing and teaching him by directing his gaze and concern toward him, while the disciple remains unaware. In reality, the vital factor is sincerity. Real shaykhs are there but, "Transcendent is He who has made the evidence that points to His saints through the evidence that points to Him, and does not allow anyone to reach them except those He wishes to make reach Him."[6]

If you want something from your shaykh, or if you have a question to ask, do not refrain out of awe and respect. Ask once, twice, and three times. Do not think that it is courteous to refrain from asking, unless of course the shaykh himself indicates that you should remain silent and leave this question, in which case you must obey.

If the shaykh prevents you from doing something, or shows preference to someone else, beware of thinking ill of him. Be convinced that he has done what is best for you and most beneficial. If you do something wrong which angers your shaykh, be quick to apologize until he again becomes pleased with you. If you suspect a change in the shaykh's feeling toward you, when for instance you find that he does not smile at you as much as he usually did, you must tell him of your fear that he has changed toward you, for it may be due to something you did, in which case you can repent. Or it may be that you only imagined the shaykh to have changed and that this was a thought thrown into your heart by the Devil so as to distress you, in which case when you find out that the shaykh is pleased with you your heart will regain its peace. This cannot happen if, rather than talking about it, you keep quiet in the knowledge that you have done nothing wrong.

When you see a disciple who is full of respect and awe for his shaykh, who believes in him and obeys him fully, outwardly and inwardly, and behaves towards him with the appropriate good manners, such a disciple will inevitably inherit his secret[7] or part of it should he survive him.

CONCLUSION
The Attributes of the Sincere Disciple and How He Should Behave

A certain gnostic, may God be pleased with him and make us benefit from him, once said, "A disciple is not one until he is able to find in the Quran everything that he wants, know the difference between diminution and increase, become independent of the servants by the grace of [his] Lord, and regard gold and dust as equal.

A disciple is one who observes limits, keeps his promises, is content with what he has, and is patient when deprived.

A disciple is one who is thankful in prosperity, patiently endures afflictions and bitter decrees, praises his Lord in ease and in hardship, and remains true to Him in private and in public.

A disciple is one who is not enslaved by other than God, nor by events; he is one who is neither vanquished by appetites nor dominated by habits. His words are invocation and wisdom, his silence reflection and heeding examples. His actions precede his words and are proof of his knowledge. His inner garment is reverence and gravity, his cloak humility and modesty. He follows truth and prefers it, and rejects falsehood and denounces it. He loves the best of people and is their ally, and he detests evil people and is their enemy. Dealing with him proves him better than what is said about him, and keeping his company proves him better than his reputation. He helps others abundantly, but his own demands are slight. He is far from frivolousness. He is honest and trustworthy. He neither lies nor betrays, and is neither a miser nor a coward. He neither insults nor curses, is not concerned with what is not his share, and is not parsimonious with what he has. What is within him is good, so are his intentions, and there is no evil in him. He is very resolute in drawing nearer to his Lord, disdainful of this world, and does not repeat his errors. Whether he acts or refrains is not due to his appetites. Loyalty and chivalry are his companions, modesty and manliness his allies. He exacts everyone's rights from himself, but never seeks to exact his rights from anyone. When he is given, he thanks, when withheld, he is patient. When he commits an injustice, he repents and asks for forgiveness. When an injustice is committed against him, he forgives and pardons.

He likes to remain unknown and hidden, and dislikes prominence and fame. He does not talk of what does not concern him, and his heart is saddened by his shortcomings. He accepts no compromise in religious matter and does not please people by displeasing the Lord of the Worlds.

He finds solace in isolation and loneliness, but estrangement in mixing with people. Whenever you meet him, you find him engaged in acts of goodness or acquiring knowledge. He is a person from whom people expect goodness and do not fear evil. He does not repay harm with harm, and does not shun those who shun him. He is like a palm tree, throwing tender dates at you when you throw stones at it; like soil on which filth is thrown, but out of which grow beautiful things.

The light of his truthfulness shows outwardly, and what is shown on his face indicates what is hidden inwardly. He strives and aspires to please his Lord, and is eager and careful to follow His Messenger, His Chosen, His Beloved, whom the disciple takes for example in all his affairs, and follows in his character, behavior, and speech, in compliance with the command of his Great Lord in His Noble Book:

> *Take what the Messenger has brought to you and refrain from what he has forbidden you.* (QURAN, 59:7)
>
> *You have in the Messenger of God a good example for whoever has hope in God and the Last Day and remembers God in abundance.* (QURAN, 33:21)
>
> *The one who obeys the Messenger obeys God.* (QURAN, 4:80)
>
> *Those who give allegiance to you are giving allegiance to God.* (QURAN, 48:10)
>
> *Say [O Muḥammad], "If you love God, follow me and God will love you and forgive your sins; God is Forgiving, Compassionate.* (QURAN, 3:31)
>
> *Let those who contravene his commands beware lest they become afflicted or stricken by a painful torment.* (QURAN, 24:63)

So you see, [the disciple] is extremely careful in following his Prophet ﷺ, obeying the command of his Lord, aspiring to the generous promise, and fleeing the threat of suffering mentioned in those verses we have just quoted and those we left out but which carry the same meaning: good tidings of utmost success to the followers of the Messenger and warnings of utmost shame and disgrace to those who disobey him!

O God! We ask You—by Your being God and there being no God but You, the Affectionate, the Bountiful, the Designer of the heavens and the earth, the Lord of Majesty and Generosity—to confer on us perfection in following Your servant and Messenger, our master Muḥammad, may God's blessings and peace be upon him, in his character, behavior, and words, outwardly and inwardly. Make us live and die according to this by Your mercy, O Most Merciful! God, our Lord, to You belongs abundant fragrant praise, as full of blessings as befits the majesty of Your Countenance and the magnitude of Your sovereignty. *"Transcendent are You, we have no knowledge save that which You taught us. You are the Knowing, the Wise"* (QURAN, 2:32). *"There is no God but You. Transcendent are You! I have been among the unjust"* (QURAN, 21:87)

This treatise is now complete. [It is guidance] for the disciple, to whom firmness, support, and right direction are granted by his Lord, the Glorious.

It was dictated—may God be praised—in seven or eight nights of Ramadan of the year 1071 of the emigration of the Prophet, may the best of God's blessings and peace be upon him. And praise belongs to God, Lord of the Worlds.

NOTES

(For Good Manners*)*

1. A *wird* is often translated as "litany," namely, a litany of supplications and phrases of remembrance of God that one says each day. But a *wird* may also be any kind of supererogatory worship that is repeated regularly, such as non-obligatory ritual prayers, recitations of the Quran, and the like.

2. *Sharīʿa* is the sacred law. To practice it with excellence and effectiveness one must have received adequate knowledge and training, both of which constitute *ṭarīqa*, the method that leads to inward purification. This method permits one to combat the lower tendencies of the soul so as to reach the state where the lights of *ḥaqīqa*, or realization, begin to shine upon the heart of the seeker. Most of the writings of Imām al-Ḥaddād are concerned with the second term of the triad, that is, the method.

3. Spiritual power (*himma*) is the shaykh's ability to influence his disciple's heart either by transmitting to him some of the lights and knowledge he has attained or raising the disciple's spiritual resolution, concentration, and eagerness for the path to God.

4. The shaykh of *taḥkīm* is the spiritual master in the fullest meaning of the word. He is the one who has power of decision over the disciple's outward and inward religious affairs.

5. The shaykh of *tabarruk* is the saint one sits with to receive some of the radiation of his *baraka* and to benefit from his prayers, knowing that they are accepted by God.

6. This is one of the *ḥikam* of Ibn ʿAṭāʾillāh.

7. The secret meant here is part of the spiritual bond between the saint and his Lord. A spiritual master may have thousands of disciples, many of which will reach God through him, so that the secrets he may bequeath to his children and successors on leaving this earth are not a necessity for reaching the end of the path, rather they are extra lights and powers contributing to the flowering of sainthood.

TRANSLATOR'S APPENDIX ONE

Sexual intercourse is conceived from three different perspectives. The usual legal manner states that since God created man with physical appetites, there cannot be anything wrong with gratifying them, as long as it is done within the legal limits set by the *Sharī'a*. They may even be raised from the status of what is merely permissible to that of what is praiseworthy and deserving of Divine reward if the proper intentions precede them. Should one intend, for example, before eating, to preserve his health to be able to worship his Lord or struggle for the cause of God, and then he or she eats without excess, observing the prescribed *sunna*s, then eating is raised in this case to the level of a devotional activity. Similarly, when one's intention in getting married is to follow the *sunna* of the Prophet ﷺ, gratify his sexual impulse in a lawful manner, obviating the temptation to resort to the illegal, to form an efficiently functioning Muslim family, which is the cornerstone of Islamic society, encourage his wife to be a good Muslim, raise his children in the manner most pleasing to God and His Messenger, and thus contribute to the stability of Muslim society and the preservation and propagation of Islam, then marriage becomes a most praiseworthy activity, deserving of Divine reward for each of these intentions. Let us not forget that the Prophet did explicitly state that lawful sexual intercourse with one's wife attracts reward in the Hereafter, just as unlawful intercourse attracts punishment. He also said that every pleasing thing he says or does, even feeding his wife with his own hand, is extremely pleasing to God.

The second view is the ascetic one, which is the one that has produced the aforementioned utterance of Imām 'Alī. The ascetic is a person who wishes to raise himself from the bestial level of those over-involved with their physical appetites to that of the angels, entirely devoid of such appetites. The language used to shock people out of their slothful slumber is appropriately abrasive and may be crude. Thus eating is said to be the activity of cattle, that is, it is disgusting, because it is followed by excretion, and blameworthy, because it leads to laziness. Sleep is said to be reprehensible because it diverts time that should be spent remembering God, which is a function of the spirit, to rest which is an unworthy function of the body. Sexual intercourse is taken out of its total context and seen only as a gratification of a bestial appetite and preoccupation with other than God, who alone should be attended to and loved.

The third and most complete view is the spiritual one. The ascetic view is expedient as a transitory stage between the first and third stages. However, the Prophet ﷺ advised his Companions to cross this stage in a moderate, not an excessive manner. When told that Abū Dardā had abandoned food, sleep, and sleeping with his wife, he said to him, "Your body has a right upon you, your family has a right upon you." Spiritual masters, including *sayyidunā* ʿAlī, attended to their families, enjoyed a warm emotional and physical relationship with their spouses, except in rare exceptional circumstances when they were overcome by a powerful spiritual state, which normally is only transitory. The spiritual view is one which allows human beings to perceive men and women as representing the two complementary poles of everything in the created universe. The more profound and thus essential view is that they represent the two complementary groups of Divine Attributes, those of Majesty and those of Beauty. The physical union of male and female is thus symbolic of the union of opposites, which occurs only in the formless world of lights, perceptible only by spiritual contemplation, never by the physical eye or the rational mind. This is partly why the Prophet stated that, of this world, only women and perfume had been made lovable to him, women being the symbol of Divine Beauty and perfume being the only pleasure that is

Translator's Appendix

not bestial, the evidence for its being a spiritual pleasure being that it is the only pleasure that angels enjoy of the physical world.

Imām ʿAlī's words must have been addressed to those who were or should have been in the ascetic transitional state between ordinary and spiritual beings. The Prophet having said, "Speak to each people according to their understanding." No statement, even in the Quran and *sunna*, except *lā ilāha illa'llāh*, should be understood in an unconditional manner. One should always look for the context, the limitations of that statement, and the possible exceptions.

TRANSLATOR'S APPENDIX TWO
Method of the "People of the Right Hand"

The Quran separates human beings into three categories: *the Drawn Near*, who include the Prophets and saints; *the Companions of the Right Hand*, the right hand side being the direction of paradise, those destined for paradise without being either Prophets or saints ranging from the virtuous to the most ordinary sinful believer; and *the Companions of the Left Hand*, the direction to the left being that of Hell (QURAN, 56). These are the disbelievers of all kinds. Sufis have used this terminology to differentiate between those who actively pursue a spiritual path; they are included with the Drawn Near, even though they may not have reached their spiritual degree. Those who have no such inclination, but are still believers—obeying most of God's injunctions, albeit with less sincerity and enthusiasm, and avoiding most of His prohibitions, albeit with not as much care as the travelers on the path—are the Companions of the Right Hand. By the time of Imām al-Ḥaddād, the classical method of the Sufis, requiring total obedience from the disciple to the master, to facilitate his guiding him along the path, saving time, and allowing for spiritual openings, had begun to become impractical, for rare had the disciples become who could endure such arduous training. Imām al-Ḥaddād started his life as a traveler on the classical path, then gradually changed over, as a master, and formulated the easier method, more suitable for the End of Time. The one point that is still mentioned in this treatise that belongs to the old method is the question of surrendering all one's affairs to the shaykh, which Imām al-Ḥaddād himself, not much later, stated was no longer to be requested. Another reason for abrogating this requirement is that the masters who deserve to be obeyed in this manner have grown fewer and fewer, until in a time such as ours, especially in the West, they are almost non-existent.

In 1411 AH, Ḥabīb Aḥmad Mashhūr al-Ḥaddād, may God be pleased with him, attended a gathering on the occasion of the anniversary of the passing of Imām al-Ḥaddād. He confined his speech that day on explaining the method used since the days of the Imām and still practiced today. He mentioned the masters of old, such as Shaykh ʿAbd al-Qādir al-Jīlānī, Shaykh Aḥmad al-Rifāʿī, and others, and said that their method imposed on the disciples to eat little, speak little, sleep little, and mix as little as possible with people. Then he remarked that even in those days, those who lived this pattern to the full were few and that their requirement that the disciple surrender to them unconditionally was difficult even then, becoming entirely impossible today, except in the rarest and most exceptional of circumstances. He spoke sarcastically of our times, in the same terms that his ancestor the Imām had used, calling them these lovely blessed times, the times of generalized sedition, deception, absurd, and downright destructive ideas and blameworthy innovations. He said that the Method of the People of the Right Hand is an easy method. It means that you perform whatever obligations and *sunna*s God has prescribed for you, tread the path of *taqwā* as best as you can, and keep the company of good people and move along with them, for he who loves some people is one of them. When you behave as they do you become one of the

Translator's Appendix

Companions of the Right Hand and you join the people of *ṭarīqa*. It is sufficient good for you to be one of them. *And whoever obeys God and the Messenger, they are with those whom God has favored, of the Prophets, the ṣiddiqūn, the martyrs, and the virtuous. And the best of companions are they!* (QURAN: 4:69). Then Ḥabīb Aḥmad stated that much of the previous self-disciplining practices have been replaced with the constant remembrance of God, recommending in particular those of Imām al-Ḥaddād, specifically, *al-Wird al-Laṭīf* and *al-Rātib*. Finally, he said a few words about *ijāza*, the permission or authorization to use these and other invocations that is transmitted from one master to the next and from master to disciple to render the use of these invocations more fruitful.